BEN BORN AGAIN'S

NEW

BELIEVER'S
GROWTH
BOOK

BY GREG LAURIE

WITH GREG LAURIE

P.O. Box 4000 ·Riverside, CA 92514-4000

Written By Greg Laurie
Design & Illustration by Rex Morache

...IT'S IMPORTANT THAT YOU OPEN YOUR BIBLE AND LOOK UP THE SCRIPTURE REFERENCES AS YOU READ THROUGH THIS BOOKLET.

FOLLOW THIS EXAMPLE- JOHN 3:16 MEANS THE BOOK OF JOHN, CHAPTER 3, VERSE 16.

I'M BEN BORN AGAIN AND THIS IS MY BUDDY, WILLIE.

WE WOULD LIKE TO HELP YOU TAKE YOUR FIRST STEPS TOWARD GROWING IN JESUS.

THESE STEPS ARE IMPORTANT FOR YOU WHETHER YOU ARE RECEIVING JESUS, MAKING A RECOMMITMENT, OR NEED FURTHER ASSURANCE OF YOUR FAITH.

A WORD OF ENCOURAGEMENT FROM
GREG LAURIE

Welcome to God's Family!

Whether you are receiving Christ as your personal Lord and Savior for the first time or rededicating your life back to Him, this can be the beginning of a new and fulfilling life for you as you follow the Lord. You may be wondering if Jesus Christ really came into your life when you prayed to receive Him.

You may have had a real emotional experience, such as great joy in realizing that your sins were forgiven, or perhaps a real sense of sorrow over all the wrong you have done. Then again, you may have felt absolutely nothing! But when you prayed that prayer of receiving Jesus Christ into your life and really meant it, He came in! God promises us in His word, *"These things I have written to you who believe in the name of the Son of God, that you may know that you have eternal life, and that you may continue to believe in the name of the Son of God" (1 Jn. 5:13).*

God has promised you that He has come into your life. You have His Word on it. That means your sin is forgiven, your past is behind you, and He has put a new spiritual nature in you. His Word tells us, *"For if a man is in Christ he*

1.

becomes a new person altogether – the past is finished and gone, everything has become fresh and new" (2 Cor. 5:17/Phillips Translation).

Your decision to receive Christ also means that you are now going to Heaven one day. That's a lot to be thankful for! Now you need to take some practical steps to grow strong spiritually. There are three basic building blocks I would recommend, and a fourth that really is an outgrowth of the first three.

1. READ THE BIBLE

I cannot emphasize this enough! The Bible says, *"All Scripture is God-breathed and is useful for teaching, rebuking, correcting and training in righteousness"* (2 Tim. 3:16 NIV). All that one needs to know about God – and for that fact, life in general – is found in the pages of Scripture. The truths in this great Book are going to come alive to you as the Author has taken residence in your heart. I recommend you start with the Gospel of John, which is the story of the life and ministry of Jesus. I would also recommend that you commit passages of Scripture to memory. The psalmist wrote, *"Your word I have hidden in my heart, that I might not sin against You"* (Psalm 119:11).

 **PRAY**

The Bible says of prayer, *"Be anxious for nothing, but in everything by prayer...let your requests be made known to God" (Phil. 4:6).* You can pray any time. Take advantage of this wonderful privilege in which you have 24-hour access to the Creator of the universe!

3. GO TO CHURCH

The Bible tells us to *"not* (forsake) *the assembling of ourselves together..." (Heb10:25).* You need the encouragement of other Christians and the teaching of God's word. If you do not know of a good Bible-teaching church in your area, write me and I will recommend one.

4. SHARE WITH OTHERS WHAT JESUS HAS DONE FOR YOU

Let others know how He has changed your life, and perhaps even invite them to come to church with you!

In closing, what you are essentially

doing now is following Jesus Christ as your Lord and Savior. Jesus said, *"Follow me,"* which literally means "to walk the same road." It also implies "to continue" in that walk. Therefore, to follow Jesus is to walk the same road with Him in a continual, consistent, ongoing manner. It should also be pointed out that the phrase, *"follow Me,"* could be better translated *"follow with Me."* In other words, Jesus is promising to be our companion and our friend as we continually and consistently walk the same road with Him.

There are no shortcuts to growing spiritually. We need to apply ourselves regularly and consistently to His word, prayer, and worshiping with other believers. You may not see the changes in your life overnight, but you will in time. The Christian life is a wonderful adventure as we get to personally know the God who made us and discover His personal plan for our lives. It also is the greatest life there is! You have made the right decision for time and eternity. Congratulations!

I encourage you to take advantage of the many resources in this booklet. God bless you.

In Jesus,

Greg Laurie

BORN AGAIN!!

God loves you and wants you to experience His peace and life.

The Bible says... *"For God so loved the world that He gave His only begotten Son, that whoever believes in Him should not perish but have everlasting life" (John 3:16).*

Being at peace with God is not automatic because you, by nature, are separated from God.

The Bible says... *"For all have sinned and fall short of the glory of God" (Romans 3:23).*

Man has tried to bridge this separation in many ways... without success.

God's love bridges the gap of separation between God and you. When Jesus Christ died on the cross and rose from the grave, He paid the penalty for your sins.

The Bible says... *"He personally carried the load of our sins in His own body when he died on the cross..." (1 Peter 2:24 TLB)*.

You cross the bridge into God's family when you receive Christ by personal invitation.

The Bible says... *"But as many as received Him, to them He gave the right to become children of God, even to those who believe in His name..." (John 1:12)*.

Jesus said, *"Behold, I stand at the door and knock. If anyone hears My voice and opens the door, I will come in..." (Revelation 3:20)*.

"For whoever calls upon the name of the Lord shall be saved" (Romans 10:13).

YOU NEED TO DO 4 THINGS TO RECEIVE CHRIST...

 ADMIT your spiritual need. *"I am a sinner."*

 REPENT and be willing to turn from your sin.

 BELIEVE that Jesus Christ died for you on the cross.

 RECEIVE, through prayer, Jesus Christ into your heart and life.

PRAY SOMETHING LIKE THIS FROM THE SINCERITY OF YOUR HEART...

Dear Lord Jesus,

I know I am a sinner. I believe you died for my sins. Right now, I turn from my sins and open the door of my heart and life. I receive you as my personal Lord and Savior. Thank you for saving me.

Amen.

WHEI E AI E YOU PLANTED?

Jesus told a story about a farmer who went out to sow some seed. The seed Jesus spoke of is the Word of God.

READ: LUKE 8:4-15. IN THIS STORY, JESUS TELLS YOU HOW TO HAVE A FRUITFUL LIFE IN HIM. IF YOU ARE MAKING A RECOMMITMENT, YOU WILL SEE WHY YOU FELL AWAY BEFORE.

PITFALLS TO AVOID!

Some seed fell by the wayside (along the path), was trampled on, and the birds ate it up. Jesus said the birds represent the devil, who steals the Word away before some really believe.

Some seed fell on rocky ground, representing those who spring up eagerly at first, but when trials and temptations come, they fall away because they have no roots.

Some seed fell among thorns. Jesus said the thorns are the worries, riches and pleasures of this life that grow up with the seed, choking out the fruit of these individuals' spiritual lives.

RICH SOIL TO GROW IN!

Other seed fell on good ground! These people are those who hear the Word and keep it, bearing much fruit with endurance.

YOUR COMMITMENT TO CHRIST IS REFLECTED IN ONE OF THESE WAYS. BE DETERMINED TO BE A FRUITFUL SEED, GROWING IN THE RICH SOIL OF GOD'S WORD!

CHANGE!

It's important that we turn from our sin (that which separates us from God). The Bible says, *"Therefore, if anyone is in Christ, he is a new creation; old things have passed away; behold, all things have become new"* (2 Cor. 5:17).

As we become new people in Jesus Christ, we should not live like unbelievers do. *"And do not be conformed to this world, but be transformed by the renewing of your mind, that you may prove what is that good and acceptable and perfect will of God"* (Romans 12:2).

We find our attitudes, desires, and, as a result, our lifestyle changing. The Apostle Paul recognized this and wrote:

"Why all this stress on behaviour? Because, as I think you have realized the present time is of the highest importance – it is time to wake up to reality. Every day brings God's salvation nearer than the day in which we took the first step of faith. The night is nearly over, the day has almost dawned. Let us therefore fling away the

things that men do in the dark, let us arm ourselves for the fight of the day! Let us live cleanly, as in the daylight, not in the delights of getting drunk or playing with sex, nor yet in quarreling or jealousies. Let us be Christ's men from head to foot, and give no chances to the flesh to have its fling" (Romans 13:11-14/Phillips Translation).

WATER BAPTISM!

Water baptism is an outward showing of an inward doing. The Bible tells us, *"Do you not know that as many of us who have been baptized into Christ Jesus were baptized into His death? Therefore, we were buried with Him through baptism into death, that just as Christ was raised from the dead by the glory of the Father, even so we also should walk in newness of life" (Romans 6:3,4).*

I HOPE
I DON'T GET
WATER UP
MY NOSE!

It's like a happy funeral! We die to our old, sinful nature as we symbolically go into a watery grave. It's also a way of publicly making a stand for Jesus.

DYNAMITE POWER!

THIS LOOKS LIKE A JOB FOR THE SPIRITUAL MAN!

13.

One thing you will find out real fast is that it's not hard to be a Christian – it's impossible! (That is, apart from the power of the Holy Spirit.)

Jesus said, *"I will ask the Father, and He will give you another Helper, that He may be with you forever"* (John 14:16 /NASB).

Jesus wants you to live your life filled with the power of the Holy Spirit.

He said, *"But you shall receive power* (dynamite) *when the Holy Spirit has come UPON you; and you shall be witnesses to Me..."* (Acts 1:8).

The only effective way to live the Christian life and be a witness for Jesus Christ is through and by the power of the Holy Spirit. You might ask Jesus to fill you with the Holy Spirit each day (Ephesians 5:18). We need all the help we can get!

READ: THE ENTIRE BOOK OF ACTS TO SEE HOW THE HOLY SPIRIT WORKED IN THE LIVES OF THOSE EARLY BELIEVERS.

4 STEPS TO GROWTH!

 # 1. PRAY!

Prayer is talking and listening to God. The Lord loves to hear from us! You can pray anytime you want to–driving your car, on your knees, wherever and whenever.

The Bible says: *"Pray without ceasing, in everything give thanks; for this is the will of God in Christ Jesus for you"* (1 Thess. 5:17-18).

"I will bless the Lord at all times; His praise shall continually be in my mouth" (Psalm 34:1).

Jesus gave us a model prayer in the Gospel of Luke 11:1-14. You can look it up and read it in your Bible.

When we sin (miss God's mark), we should immediately confess our sins, for He is faithful and just to forgive us from all unrighteousness (1 John 1:9).

READ: PHILIPPIANS 4:6, JUDE 20, LUKE 18:1, ISAIAH 55:6, ECCLESIASTES 5:2, LUKE 11:5-13 AND PSALM 145:18

I VALUE
GOD'S WORD
MORE THAN
MY FOOD*

*Job 23:12

2. STUDY

The Bible is like spiritual food. Just as you clothe and feed your physical body, you must clothe and feed your spiritual body. The Bible says...

"Do your best to present yourself to God as one approved, a workman who does not need to be ashamed and who correctly handles the word of truth" (2 Timothy 2:15/NIV).

It is good to take a portion of Scripture (a book of the Bible, a topic, etc.)

and study it. If you are reading the Bible for the first time, you might start with the Gospel of John.

SEE GOSPEL OF JOHN AND DAILY READING SCHEDULE ON PAGE 34. IT IS ALSO GOOD TO MEMORIZE SCRIPTURE ... SEE PAGE 29.

"His (the godly man's) delight is in the law of the Lord, and in His law he meditates day and night." (Psalm 1:2)

"Your Word I have hidden in my heart that I might not sin against you." (Psalm 119:11)

In Ephesians 6:17, the Apostle Paul says, *"And take the sword of the spirit, which is the word of God."* As Satan will tempt you to disobey God's Word, the Scriptures are an offensive weapon you can use against the temptation of Satan (read Luke 4:1-14). When Jesus was tempted, He replied with Scripture.

SEE PAGE 23 TO 25 ON TEMPTATIONS.

The Bible tells us, *"But be doers of the word, and not hearers only, deceiving yourselves"* (James 1:22).

We must practice what is taught in God's Word. Jesus said, *"If you love Me, keep My commandments"* (John 14:15).

So, open your Bibles, dig in, and have a spiritual feast!

READ: PSALM 119:1-176, LUKE 11:28, JOHN 8:31, HEBREWS 10:7, 1PETER 2:2 AND 2PETER 1:4

3. FELLOWSHIP

The Bible tells us we need to have fellowship one with another. The word fellowship means *"a joint participation of things held in common by both."* In Hebrews 10:24-25, it says:

"Let us consider how to stimulate one another to love and good deeds, not forsaking our own assembling together, as is the habit of some, but encouraging one another, and all the more, as you see the day drawing near." (NAS translation)

You might compare fellowship to a heap of burning coals. If you separate one piece of coal from the others, it will get cold and die.

READ: ACTS 2:42-47,
EPHESIANS 5:2, 19, 30,
HEBREWS 3:13,
1PETER 3:8 AND 1JOHN 4:7

4. WITNESS

As a result of praying, reading your Bible, and having fellowship, which are all taking in, you'll want to start giving out! The way to do this is to witness.

Jesus said, *"Go into all the world and preach the gospel* (good news) *to every creature"* (*Mark 16:15*).

The Bible teaches, *"It is appointed for men to die once, but after this the judgment"* (*Hebrews 9:27; see also Revelation 20:11-13*).

We must realize that people's souls are on the very balance of eternity! We, as God's representatives, must share the "Good News" that Jesus loves them and died on the cross that their sins might be forgiven and that they might have abundant and eternal life.

As we learned about the power of the Holy Spirit (back on pages 13 & 14), we read that He gives us dynamite power to be a witness for Jesus.

So, now that you've received that power, go and live, telling others how they, too, can have a new life in Jesus Christ!

EXTRA, EXTRA!

READ ALL ABOUT IT !!!

TEMPTATION & TRIALS

As a result of growing spiritually as a Christian, you're going to experience what the Bible calls trials.

"In this you greatly rejoice, though now for a little while, if need be, you have been grieved by various trials, that the genuineness of your faith, being much more precious than gold that perishes, though it is tested by fire, may be found to praise, honor, and glory at the revelation of Jesus Christ." (1 Peter 1:6-7)

There will be times in your Christian walk when you will not feel the presence of God. But our Christian walk should not be based on feelings; it should be based on faith (read Hebrews 11). It is important to learn what the Lord is trying to teach us through these trials.

READ: JAMES 1:1-4, HEBREWS 12 AND 1 PETER 4:12

TEMPTATIONS!

Now that you're serving the Lord, Satan is going to try to draw you away, tempting you to disobey God's Word. It is not a sin to be tempted, for even Jesus was tempted (Luke 4). It only becomes sin when we give in to that temptation. God will never let a temptation become so strong that we can't handle it.

"No temptation has overtaken you except such as is common to man; but God is faithful, who will not allow you to be tempted beyond what you are able, but with the temptation will also make the way of escape, that you may be able to bear it."
(1 Corinthians 10:13)

24.

The Bible gives us a formula for dealing with Satan's temptations.

"Therefore submit to God. Resist the devil and he will flee from you." (James 4:7 NKJ)

There are **"3'R'S"** that will help you to deal with temptation.

1. REALIZE...
WHO'S TEMPTING YOU (SATAN).

2. RESIST...
THE DEVIL; HE WILL FLEE FROM YOU.

3. REJOICE...
THE VICTORY IS YOURS IN JESUS !

READ: MATTHEW 13:22, 26:41,
ROMANS 6:12,
ROMANS 8:35 AND
EPHESIANS 6:11-17

GOD'S WILL!

As Christians, it is very important that we know God's will for our lives. Jesus wants to guide us and speak to us! To know God's choice, we must hear His voice. It's important to know that God will usually speak in the spiritual realm, so you must listen with your spiritual ears. Jesus said that His *"sheep"* (those who follow Christ) hear His voice (John 10:4).

In the book of 1 Kings, the 19th chapter, a prophet of the Lord named Elijah was waiting to hear God's voice. And God spoke to him in a still, small voice. Likewise, God will sometimes speak to us in a *"still, small voice."* We just must learn to listen for it.

At the same time, however, Satan will often try to deceive us into thinking we are hearing God's voice when it's really a counterfeit. For that reason, we must test all voices with God's lie detector:

THE BIBLE!

Here are **3** basic ways to know God's will:

1. THE BIBLE: God will never contradict the Bible (Acts 17:11). Go to the Scriptures in times of decision. Remember to read the Word of God in context.

2. THE PEACE OF GOD: *"And let the peace* (soul harmony which comes) *from the Christ rule* (act as umpire continually) *in your hearts–deciding and settling with finality all questions that arise in your minds–*[in that peaceful state] *to which* [as members of Christ's] *one body you were also called* [to live]. *And be thankful–appreciative, giving praise to God always" (Colossians 3:15 /Amplified Bible).*

3. CIRCUMSTANCES: Outward things will fall into place as God leads you. (But remember, make your decisions primarily upon the principles given in God's Word.)

ABIDING IN CHRIST!

In John's gospel, Jesus said, *"If you abide in Me, and My words abide in you, You will ask what you desire, and it shall be done for you."* (John 15:7)

What a promise! The word "abide" means: "a permanence of position, maintaining unbroken fellowship with another." We need to sink our spiritual roots deep into the Lord; besides being our Heavenly Father, He wants to be our closest friend! Jesus said, *"Abide in Me, and I in you. As the branch cannot bear fruit of itself, unless it abides in the vine, neither can you, unless you abide in Me"* (John 15:4).

The "fruit" Jesus is speaking of is defined in Galatians 5:22: *"But the fruit of the Spirit is love, joy, peace, longsuffering, kindness, goodness, faithfulness."*

The Bible also tells us that whoever continually abides in Him will not continually sin (1 John 3:6).

Apart from Jesus Christ we can do nothing! But, when we abide in Christ, we can say with the Apostle Paul, *"I can do all things through Christ who strengthens me"* *(Philippians 4:13).*

HOW TO MEMORIZE:

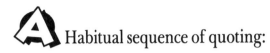 Habitual sequence of quoting:

**1. THE TOPIC 2. THE REFERENCE
3. THE VERSE 4. THE REFERENCE**

The reference is normally more difficult to remember than the verse. That is why it should be repeated before and after the verse. The reference is like the handle on a suitcase, enabling you to lift up a complete portion from the Bible whenever needed.

The real secret of Scripture memory is review, review, review. "Either use it or lose it." Remember the verses as you remember a telephone number. Remember how you memorized telephone numbers? You dialed, Dialed, DIALED! You can memorize by review, Review, REVIEW!

Quote the verse aloud. Pray over the verse, asking God to make the meaning clear and applicable to you. Memorize one phrase at a time, using the reference, adding phrase by phrase until the entire verse is committed to memory.

BIBLE MEMORY VERSES

PROMISE OF FORGIVENESS

1 John 1:9 NKJV

"If we confess our sins, He is faithful and just to forgive us our sins and to cleanse us from all unrighteousness."

VICTORY THROUGH THE WORD

Psalms 119:9,11 NKJV

"How can a young man cleanse his way? By taking heed according to Your word. Your word I have hidden in my heart, that I might not sin against You."

FISHERS OF MEN

Matthew 4:19 NKJV

And He said to them, "Follow Me, and I will make you fishers of men."

APPLYING HIS WORD

Joshua 1:8 NKJV

"This Book of the Law shall not depart from your mouth, but you shall meditate in it day and night, that you may observe to do according to all that is written in it. For then you will make your way prosperous, and then you will have good success."

MORE MEMORY VERSES

PROMISE OF SALVATION

John 3:16 NKJV

"For God so loved the world that He gave His only begotten Son, that whoever believes in Him should not perish but have everlasting life."

SHARE CHRIST

Acts 1:8

"But you shall receive power when the Holy Spirit has come upon you; and you shall be witnesses to Me in Jerusalem, and in all Judea and Samaria, and to the end of the earth."

CONFIDENCE IN PRAYER

1 John 5:14,15 NKJV

"Now this is the confidence that we have in Him, that if we ask anything according to His will, He hears us. And if we know that He hears us, whatever we ask, we know that we have the petitions that we have asked of Him."

PROOF OF LOVE

John 14:21 NKJV

"He who has My commandments and keeps them, it is he who loves me. And he who loves me will be loved by My Father, and I will love him and manifest Myself to him."

THE GOSPEL OF JOHN

32.

DAILY BIBLE READING

BEGIN TODAY TO READ
PART OF JOHN'S GOSPEL,
AND CHECK OFF EACH
PORTION AS YOU FINISH IT.

____ Day 22 John 18:1-14 · Arrest of Jesus

____ Day 23 John 18:15-27 · Peter Denies Jesus

____ Day 24 John 18:28-40 · Jesus Before Pilate

____ Day 25 John 19:1-15 · Jesus is Condemned

____ Day 26 John 19:16-30 · The Crucifixion

____ Day 27 John 19:31-42 · Jesus is Buried

____ Day 28 John 20:1-18 · The Resurrection

____ Day 29 John 20:19-31 · Jesus Appears

____ Day 30 John 21 · Events Following Resurrection

JOHN 1

THE ETERNAL WORD

1 In the beginning was the Word, and the Word was with God, and the Word was God.
2 He was in the beginning with God.
3 All things were made through Him, and without Him nothing was made that was made.
4 In Him was life, and the life was the light of men.
5 And the light shines in the darkness, and the darkness did not comprehend it.

JOHN'S WITNESS: THE TRUE LIGHT

6 There was a man sent from God, whose name was John.
7 This man came for a witness, to bear witness of the Light, that all through him might believe.
8 He was not that Light, but was sent to bear witness of that Light.
9 That was the true Light which gives light to every man who comes into the world.
10 He was in the world, and the world was made through Him, and the world did not know Him.
11 He came to His own, and His own did not receive Him.
12 But as many as received Him, to them He

gave the right to become children of God, even to those who believe in His name:

13   who were born, not of blood, nor of the will of the flesh, nor of the will of man, but of God.

THE WORD BECOMES FLESH

14   And the Word became flesh and dwelt among us, and we beheld His glory, the glory as of the only begotten of the Father, full of grace and truth.

15   John bore witness of Him and cried out, saying, "This was He of whom I said, 'He who comes after me is preferred before me, for He was before me.'"

16   And of His fullness we have all received, and grace for grace.

17   For the law was given through Moses, but grace and truth came through Jesus Christ.

18   No one has seen God at any time. The only begotten Son, who is in the bosom of the Father, He has declared Him.

A VOICE IN THE WILDERNESS

19   Now this is the testimony of John, when the Jews sent priests and Levites from Jerusalem to ask him, "Who are you?"

20   He confessed, and did not deny, but confessed, "I am not the Christ."

21   And they asked him, "What then? Are you Elijah?" He said, "I am not." "Are you the Prophet?" And he answered, "No."

22   Then they said to him, "Who are you, that we may give an answer to those who sent us? What do you say about yourself?"

23   He said: "I am 'The voice of one crying in

the wilderness: "Make straight the way of the Lord,"' as the prophet Isaiah said."

24   Now those who were sent were from the Pharisees.

25   And they asked him, saying, "Why then do you baptize if you are not the Christ, nor Elijah, nor the Prophet?"

26   John answered them, saying, "I baptize with water, but there stands One among you whom you do not know.

27   "It is He who, coming after me, is preferred before me, whose sandal strap I am not worthy to loose."

28   These things were done in Bethabara beyond the Jordan, where John was baptizing.

THE LAMB OF GOD

29   The next day John saw Jesus coming toward him, and said, "Behold! The Lamb of God who takes away the sin of the world!

30   "This is He of whom I said, 'After me comes a Man who is preferred before me, for He was before me.'

31   "I did not know Him; but that He should be revealed to Israel, therefore I came baptizing with water."

32   And John bore witness, saying, "I saw the Spirit descending from heaven like a dove, and He remained upon Him.

33   "I did not know Him, but He who sent me to baptize with water said to me, 'Upon whom you see the Spirit descending, and remaining on Him, this is He who baptizes with the Holy Spirit.'

34   "And I have seen and testified that this is the Son of God."

THE FIRST DISCIPLES

35   Again, the next day, John stood with two of his disciples.

36   And looking at Jesus as He walked, he said, "Behold the Lamb of God!"

37   The two disciples heard him speak, and they followed Jesus.

38   Then Jesus turned, and seeing them following, said to them, "What do you seek?" They said to Him, "Rabbi" (which is to say, when translated, Teacher), "where are You staying?"

39   He said to them, "Come and see." They came and saw where He was staying, and remained with Him that day (now it was about the tenth hour).

40   One of the two who heard John speak, and followed Him, was Andrew, Simon Peter's brother.

41   He first found his own brother Simon, and said to him, "We have found the Messiah" (which is translated, the Christ).

42   And he brought him to Jesus. Now when Jesus looked at him, He said, "You are Simon the son of Jonah. You shall be called Cephas" (which is translated, A Stone).

PHILIP AND NATHANAEL

43   The following day Jesus wanted to go to Galilee, and He found Philip and said to him, "Follow Me."

44   Now Philip was from Bethsaida, the city of Andrew and Peter.

45   Philip found Nathanael and said to him, "We have found Him of whom Moses in the law, and also the prophets, wrote—Jesus of Nazareth, the son of Joseph."

46 And Nathanael said to him, "Can anything good come out of Nazareth?" Philip said to him, "Come and see."

47 Jesus saw Nathanael coming toward Him, and said of him, "Behold, an Israelite indeed, in whom is no guile!"

48 Nathanael said to Him, "How do You know me?" Jesus answered and said to him, "Before Philip called you, when you were under the fig tree, I saw you."

49 Nathanael answered and said to Him, "Rabbi, You are the Son of God! You are the King of Israel!"

50 Jesus answered and said to him, "Because I said to you, 'I saw you under the fig tree,' do you believe? You will see greater things than these."

51 And He said to him, "Most assuredly, I say to you, hereafter you shall see heaven open, and the angels of God ascending and descending upon the Son of Man."

JOHN 2

WATER TURNED TO WINE

1 On the third day there was a wedding in Cana of Galilee, and the mother of Jesus was there.

2 Now both Jesus and His disciples were invited to the wedding.

3 And when they ran out of wine, the mother of Jesus said to Him, "They have no wine."

4 Jesus said to her, "Woman, what does your concern have to do with Me? My hour has not yet come."

5 His mother said to the servants, "Whatever

He says to you, do it."

6   Now there were set there six waterpots of stone, according to the manner of purification of the Jews, containing twenty or thirty gallons apiece.

7   Jesus said to them, "Fill the waterpots with water." And they filled them up to the brim.

8   And He said to them, "Draw some out now, and take it to the master of the feast." And they took it.

9   When the master of the feast had tasted the water that was made wine, and did not know where it came from (but the servants who had drawn the water knew), the master of the feast called the bridegroom.

10   And he said to him, "Every man at the beginning sets out the good wine, and when the guests have well drunk, then that which is inferior; but you have kept the good wine until now."

11   This beginning of signs Jesus did in Cana of Galilee, and manifested His glory; and His disciples believed in Him.

12   After this He went down to Capernaum, He, His mother, His brothers, and His disciples; and they did not stay there many days.

JESUS CLEANSES THE TEMPLE

13   Now the Passover of the Jews was at hand, and Jesus went up to Jerusalem.

14   And He found in the temple those who sold oxen and sheep and doves, and the moneychangers doing business.

15   When He had made a whip of cords, He drove them all out of the temple, with the sheep and the oxen, and poured out the changers' money and overturned the tables.

16   And He said to those who sold doves, "Take these things away! Do not make My Father's house a house of merchandise!"

17   Then His disciples remembered that it was written, "Zeal for Your house has eaten Me up."

18   So the Jews answered and said to Him, "What sign do You show to us, since You do these things?"

19   Jesus answered and said to them, "Destroy this temple, and in three days I will raise it up."

20   Then the Jews said, "It has taken forty-six years to build this temple, and will You raise it up in three days?"

21   But He was speaking of the temple of His body.

22   Therefore, when He had risen from the dead, His disciples remembered that He had said this to them; and they believed the Scripture and the word which Jesus had said.

THE DISCERNER OF HEARTS

23   Now when He was in Jerusalem at the Passover, during the feast, many believed in His name when they saw the signs which He did.

24   But Jesus did not commit Himself to them, because He knew all men,

25   and had no need that anyone should testify of man, for He knew what was in man.

JOHN 3

THE NEW BIRTH

1   There was a man of the Pharisees named Nicodemus, a ruler of the Jews.

2   This man came to Jesus by night and said to Him, "Rabbi, we know that You are a teacher come from God; for no one can do these signs that You do unless God is with him."

3   Jesus answered and said to him, "Most assuredly, I say to you, unless one is born again, he cannot see the kingdom of God."

4   Nicodemus said to Him, "How can a man be born when he is old? Can he enter a second time into his mother's womb and be born?"

5   Jesus answered, "Most assuredly, I say to you, unless one is born of water and the Spirit, he cannot enter the kingdom of God.

6   "That which is born of the flesh is flesh, and that which is born of the Spirit is spirit.

7   "Do not marvel that I said to you, 'You must be born again.'

8   "The wind blows where it wishes, and you hear the sound of it, but cannot tell where it comes from and where it goes. So is everyone who is born of the Spirit."

9   Nicodemus answered and said to Him, "How can these things be?"

10   Jesus answered and said to him, "Are you the teacher of Israel, and do not know these things?

11   "Most assuredly, I say to you, We speak what We know and testify what We have seen, and you do not receive Our witness.

12   "If I have told you earthly things and you

do not believe, how will you believe if I tell you heavenly things?

13 "No one has ascended to heaven but He who came down from heaven, that is, the Son of Man who is in heaven.

14 "And as Moses lifted up the serpent in the wilderness, even so must the Son of Man be lifted up,

15 "that whoever believes in Him should not perish but have eternal life.

16 "For God so loved the world that He gave His only begotten Son, that whoever believes in Him should not perish but have everlasting life.

17 "For God did not send His Son into the world to condemn the world, but that the world through Him might be saved.

18 "He who believes in Him is not condemned; but he who does not believe is condemned already, because he has not believed in the name of the only begotten Son of God.

19 "And this is the condemnation, that the light has come into the world, and men loved darkness rather than light, because their deeds were evil.

20 "For everyone practicing evil hates the light and does not come to the light, lest his deeds should be exposed.

21 "But he who does the truth comes to the light, that his deeds may be clearly seen, that they have been done in God."

JOHN THE BAPTIST EXALTS CHRIST

22 After these things Jesus and His disciples came into the land of Judea, and there He remained with them and baptized.

23 Now John also was baptizing in Aenon near Salim, because there was much water there. And they came and were baptized.

24 For John had not yet been thrown into prison.

25 Then there arose a dispute between some of John's disciples and the Jews about purification.

26 And they came to John and said to him, "Rabbi, He who was with you beyond the Jordan, to whom you have testified—behold, He is baptizing, and all are coming to Him!"

27 John answered and said, "A man can receive nothing unless it has been given to him from heaven.

28 "You yourselves bear me witness, that I said, 'I am not the Christ,' but, 'I have been sent before Him.'

29 "He who has the bride is the bridegroom; but the friend of the bridegroom, who stands and hears him, rejoices greatly because of the bridegroom's voice. Therefore this joy of mine is fulfilled.

30 "He must increase, but I must decrease.

31 "He who comes from above is above all; he who is of the earth is earthly and speaks of the earth. He who comes from heaven is above all.

32 "And what He has seen and heard, that He testifies; and no one receives His testimony.

33 "He who has received His testimony has certified that God is true.

34 "For He whom God has sent speaks the words of God, for God does not give the Spirit by measure.

35 "The Father loves the Son, and has given all things into His hand.

36 "He who believes in the Son has everlasting

life; and he who does not believe the Son shall not see life, but the wrath of God abides on him."

JOHN 4

A SAMARITAN WOMAN MEETS HER MESSIAH

1 Therefore, when the Lord knew that the Pharisees had heard that Jesus made and baptized more disciples than John

2 (though Jesus Himself did not baptize, but His disciples),

3 He left Judea and departed again to Galilee.

4 But He needed to go through Samaria.

5 So He came to a city of Samaria which is called Sychar, near the plot of ground that Jacob gave to his son Joseph.

6 Now Jacob's well was there. Jesus therefore, being wearied from His journey, sat thus by the well. It was about the sixth hour.

7 A woman of Samaria came to draw water. Jesus said to her, "Give Me a drink."

8 For His disciples had gone away into the city to buy food.

9 Then the woman of Samaria said to Him, "How is it that You, being a Jew, ask a drink from me, a Samaritan woman?" For Jews have no dealings with Samaritans.

10 Jesus answered and said to her, "If you knew the gift of God, and who it is who says to you, 'Give Me a drink,' you would have asked Him, and He would have given you living water."

11   The woman said to Him, "Sir, You have nothing to draw with, and the well is deep. Where then do You get that living water?

12   "Are You greater than our father Jacob, who gave us the well, and drank from it himself, as well as his sons and his livestock?"

13   Jesus answered and said to her, "Whoever drinks of this water will thirst again,

14   "but whoever drinks of the water that I shall give him will never thirst. But the water that I shall give him will become in him a fountain of water springing up into everlasting life."

15   The woman said to Him, "Sir, give me this water, that I may not thirst, nor come here to draw."

16   Jesus said to her, "Go, call your husband, and come here."

17   The woman answered and said, "I have no husband." Jesus said to her, "You have well said, 'I have no husband,'

18   "for you have had five husbands, and the one whom you now have is not your husband; in that you spoke truly."

19   The woman said to Him, "Sir, I perceive that You are a prophet.

20   "Our fathers worshiped on this mountain, and you Jews say that in Jerusalem is the place where one ought to worship."

21   Jesus said to her, "Woman, believe Me, the hour is coming when you will neither on this mountain, nor in Jerusalem, worship the Father.

22   "You worship what you do not know; we know what we worship, for salvation is of the Jews.

23   "But the hour is coming, and now is, when the true worshipers will worship the Father in spirit and truth; for the Father is seeking such to worship Him.

24 "God is Spirit, and those who worship Him must worship in spirit and truth."

25 The woman said to Him, "I know that Messiah is coming" (who is called Christ). "When He comes, He will tell us all things."

26 Jesus said to her, "I who speak to you am He."

THE WHITENED HARVEST

27 And at this point His disciples came, and they marveled that He talked with a woman; yet no one said, "What do You seek?" or, "Why are You talking with her?"

28 The woman then left her waterpot, went her way into the city, and said to the men,

29 "Come, see a Man who told me all things that I ever did. Could this be the Christ?"

30 Then they went out of the city and came to Him.

31 In the meantime His disciples urged Him, saying, "Rabbi, eat."

32 But He said to them, "I have food to eat of which you do not know."

33 Therefore the disciples said to one another, "Has anyone brought Him anything to eat?"

34 Jesus said to them, "My food is to do the will of Him who sent Me, and to finish His work.

35 "Do you not say, 'There are still four months and then comes the harvest'? Behold, I say to you, lift up your eyes and look at the fields, for they are already white for harvest!

36 "And he who reaps receives wages, and gathers fruit for eternal life, that both he who sows and he who reaps may rejoice together.

37 "For in this the saying is true: 'One sows and

another reaps.'

38 "I sent you to reap that for which you have not labored; others have labored, and you have entered into their labors."

THE SAVIOR OF THE WORLD

39 And many of the Samaritans of that city believed in Him because of the word of the woman who testified, "He told me all that I ever did."

40 So when the Samaritans had come to Him, they urged Him to stay with them; and He stayed there two days.

41 And many more believed because of His own word.

42 Then they said to the woman, "Now we believe, not because of what you said, for we have heard for ourselves and know that this is indeed the Christ, the Savior of the world."

WELCOME AT GALILEE

43 Now after the two days He departed from there and went to Galilee.

44 For Jesus Himself testified that a prophet has no honor in his own country.

45 So when He came to Galilee, the Galileans received Him, having seen all the things He did in Jerusalem at the feast; for they also had gone to the feast.

A NOBLEMAN'S SON HEALED

46 So Jesus came again to Cana of Galilee where He had made the water wine. And there was a certain nobleman whose son was sick at Capernaum.

47 When he heard that Jesus had come out of Judea into Galilee, he went to Him and implored Him to come down and heal his son, for he was at the point of death.

48 Then Jesus said to him, "Unless you people see signs and wonders, you will by no means believe."

49 The nobleman said to Him, "Sir, come down before my child dies!"

50 Jesus said to him, "Go your way; your son lives." So the man believed the word that Jesus spoke to him, and he went his way.

51 And as he was now going down, his servants met him and told him, saying, "Your son lives!"

52 Then he inquired of them the hour when he got better. And they said to him, "Yesterday at the seventh hour the fever left him."

53 So the father knew that it was at the same hour in which Jesus said to him, "Your son lives." And he himself believed, and his whole household.

54 This again is the second sign that Jesus did when He had come out of Judea into Galilee.

JOHN 5

A MAN HEALED AT THE POOL OF BETHESDA

1 After this there was a feast of the Jews, and Jesus went up to Jerusalem.

2 Now there is in Jerusalem by the Sheep Gate a pool, which is called in Hebrew, Bethesda, having five porches.

3 In these lay a great multitude of sick people,

blind, lame, paralyzed, waiting for the moving of the water.

4   For an angel went down at a certain time into the pool and stirred up the water; then whoever stepped in first, after the stirring of the water, was made well of whatever disease he had.

5   Now a certain man was there who had an infirmity thirty-eight years.

6   When Jesus saw him lying there, and knew that he already had been in that condition a long time, He said to him, "Do you want to be made well?"

7   The sick man answered Him, "Sir, I have no man to put me into the pool when the water is stirred up; but while I am coming, another steps down before me."

8   Jesus said to him, "Rise, take up your bed and walk."

9   And immediately the man was made well, took up his bed, and walked. And that day was the Sabbath.

10   The Jews therefore said to him who was cured, "It is the Sabbath; it is not lawful for you to carry your bed."

11   He answered them, "He who made me well said to me, 'Take up your bed and walk.'"

12   Then they asked him, "Who is the Man who said to you, 'Take up your bed and walk'?"

13   But the one who was healed did not know who it was, for Jesus had withdrawn, a multitude being in that place.

14   Afterward Jesus found him in the temple, and said to him, "See, you have been made well. Sin no more, lest a worse thing come upon you."

15   The man departed and told the Jews that it was Jesus who had made him well.

HONOR THE FATHER AND THE SON

16 For this reason the Jews persecuted Jesus, and sought to kill Him, because He had done these things on the Sabbath.

17 But Jesus answered them, "My Father has been working until now, and I have been working."

18 Therefore the Jews sought all the more to kill Him, because He not only broke the Sabbath, but also said that God was His Father, making Himself equal with God.

19 Then Jesus answered and said to them, "Most assuredly, I say to you, the Son can do nothing of Himself, but what He sees the Father do; for whatever He does, the Son also does in like manner.

20 "For the Father loves the Son, and shows Him all things that He Himself does; and He will show Him greater works than these, that you may marvel.

21 "For as the Father raises the dead and gives life to them, even so the Son gives life to whom He will.

22 "For the Father judges no one, but has committed all judgment to the Son,

23 "that all should honor the Son just as they honor the Father. He who does not honor the Son does not honor the Father who sent Him.

LIFE AND JUDGMENT ARE THROUGH THE SON

24 "Most assuredly, I say to you, he who hears My word and believes in Him who sent Me has everlasting life, and shall not come into judgment, but has passed from death into life.

25 "Most assuredly, I say to you, the hour is coming, and now is, when the dead will hear the voice of the Son of God; and those who hear will live.

26 "For as the Father has life in Himself, so He has granted the Son to have life in Himself,

27 "and has given Him authority to execute judgment also, because He is the Son of Man.

28 "Do not marvel at this; for the hour is coming in which all who are in the graves will hear His voice

29 "and come forth—those who have done good, to the resurrection of life, and those who have done evil, to the resurrection of condemnation.

30 "I can of Myself do nothing. As I hear, I judge; and My judgment is righteous, because I do not seek My own will but the will of the Father who sent Me.

THE FOURFOLD WITNESS

31 "If I bear witness of Myself, My witness is not true.

32 "There is another who bears witness of Me, and I know that the witness which He witnesses of Me is true.

33 "You have sent to John, and he has bore witness to the truth.

34 "Yet I do not receive testimony from man, but I say these things that you may be saved.

35 "He was the burning and shining lamp, and you were willing for a time to rejoice in his light.

36 "But I have a greater witness than John's; for the works which the Father has given Me to finish—the very works that I do—bear witness of Me, that the Father has sent Me.

37 "And the Father Himself, who sent Me, has testified of Me. You have neither heard His voice at any time, nor seen His form.

38 "But you do not have His word abiding in you, because whom He sent, Him you do not believe.

39 "You search the Scriptures, for in them you think you have eternal life; and these are they which testify of Me.

40 "But you are not willing to come to Me that you may have life.

41 "I do not receive honor from men.

42 "But I know you, that you do not have the love of God in you.

43 "I have come in My Father's name, and you do not receive Me; if another comes in his own name, him you will receive.

44 "How can you believe, who receive honor from one another, and do not seek the honor that comes from the only God?

45 "Do not think that I shall accuse you to the Father; there is one who accuses you—Moses, in whom you trust.

46 "For if you believed Moses, you would believe Me; for he wrote about Me.

47 "But if you do not believe his writings, how will you believe My words?"

JOHN 6

FEEDING THE FIVE THOUSAND

1 After these things Jesus went over the Sea of Galilee, which is the Sea of Tiberias.

2   Then a great multitude followed Him, because they saw His signs which He performed on those who were diseased.

3   And Jesus went up on a mountain, and there He sat with His disciples.

4   Now the Passover, a feast of the Jews, was near.

5   Then Jesus lifted up His eyes, and seeing a great multitude coming toward Him, He said to Philip, "Where shall we buy bread, that these may eat?"

6   But this He said to test him, for He Himself knew what He would do.

7   Philip answered Him, "Two hundred denarii worth of bread is not sufficient for them, that every one of them may have a little."

8   One of His disciples, Andrew, Simon Peter's brother, said to Him,

9   "There is a lad here who has five barley loaves and two small fish, but what are they among so many?"

10   Then Jesus said, "Make the people sit down." Now there was much grass in the place. So the men sat down, in number about five thousand.

11   And Jesus took the loaves, and when He had given thanks He distributed them to the disciples, and the disciples to those sitting down; and likewise of the fish, as much as they wanted.

12   So when they were filled, He said to His disciples, "Gather up the fragments that remain, so that nothing is lost."

13   Therefore they gathered them up, and filled twelve baskets with the fragments of the five barley loaves which were left over by those who had eaten.

14   Then those men, when they had seen the

sign that Jesus did, said, "This is truly the Prophet who is to come into the world."

JESUS WALKS ON THE SEA

15   Therefore when Jesus perceived that they were about to come and take Him by force to make Him king, He departed again to a mountain by Himself alone.

16   And when evening came, His disciples went down to the sea,

17   got into the boat, and went over the sea toward Capernaum. And it was now dark, and Jesus had not come to them.

18   Then the sea arose because a great wind was blowing.

19   So when they had rowed about three or four miles, they saw Jesus walking on the sea and drawing near the boat; and they were afraid.

20   But He said to them, "It is I; do not be afraid."

21   Then they willingly received Him into the boat, and immediately the boat was at the land where they were going.

THE BREAD FROM HEAVEN

22   On the following day, when the people who were standing on the other side of the sea saw that there was no other boat there, except that one which His disciples had entered, and that Jesus had not entered the boat with His disciples, but His disciples had gone away alone—

23   however, other boats came from Tiberias, near the place where they ate bread after the Lord had given thanks—

24 when the people therefore saw that Jesus was not there, nor His disciples, they also got into boats and came to Capernaum, seeking Jesus.

25 And when they found Him on the other side of the sea, they said to Him, "Rabbi, when did You come here?"

26 Jesus answered them and said, "Most assuredly, I say to you, you seek Me, not because you saw the signs, but because you ate of the loaves and were filled.

27 "Do not labor for the food which perishes, but for the food which endures to everlasting life, which the Son of Man will give you, because God the Father has set His seal on Him."

28 Then they said to Him, "What shall we do, that we may work the works of God?"

29 Jesus answered and said to them, "This is the work of God, that you believe in Him whom He sent."

30 Therefore they said to Him, "What sign will You perform then, that we may see it and believe You? What work will You do?

31 "Our fathers ate the manna in the desert; as it is written, 'He gave them bread from heaven to eat.' "

32 Then Jesus said to them, "Most assuredly, I say to you, Moses did not give you the bread from heaven, but My Father gives you the true bread from heaven.

33 "For the bread of God is He who comes down from heaven and gives life to the world."

34 Then they said to Him, "Lord, give us this bread always."

35 And Jesus said to them, "I am the bread of life. He who comes to Me shall never hunger, and he who believes in Me shall never thirst.

36 "But I said to you that you have seen Me

and yet do not believe.

37 "All that the Father gives Me will come to Me, and the one who comes to Me I will by no means cast out.

38 "For I have come down from heaven, not to do My own will, but the will of Him who sent Me.

39 "This is the will of the Father who sent Me, that of all He has given Me I should lose nothing, but should raise it up at the last day.

40 "And this is the will of Him who sent Me, that everyone who sees the Son and believes in Him may have everlasting life; and I will raise him up at the last day."

REJECTED BY HIS OWN

41 The Jews then murmured against Him, because He said, "I am the bread which came down from heaven."

42 And they said, "Is not this Jesus, the son of Joseph, whose father and mother we know? How is it then that He says, 'I have come down from heaven'?"

43 Jesus therefore answered and said to them, "Do not murmur among yourselves.

44 "No one can come to Me unless the Father who sent Me draws him; and I will raise him up at the last day.

45 "It is written in the prophets, 'And they shall all be taught by God.' Therefore everyone who has heard and learned from the Father comes to Me.

46 "Not that anyone has seen the Father, except He who is from God; He has seen the Father.

47 "Most assuredly, I say to you, he who believes in Me has everlasting life.

48 "I am the bread of life.

49   "Your fathers ate the manna in the wilderness, and are dead.

50   "This is the bread which comes down from heaven, that one may eat of it and not die.

51   "I am the living bread which came down from heaven. If anyone eats of this bread, he will live forever; and the bread that I shall give is My flesh, which I shall give for the life of the world."

52   The Jews therefore quarreled among themselves, saying, "How can this Man give us His flesh to eat?"

53   Then Jesus said to them, "Most assuredly, I say to you, unless you eat the flesh of the Son of Man and drink His blood, you have no life in you.

54   "Whoever eats My flesh and drinks My blood has eternal life, and I will raise him up at the last day.

55   "For My flesh is food indeed, and My blood is drink indeed.

56   "He who eats My flesh and drinks My blood abides in Me, and I in him.

57   "As the living Father sent Me, and I live because of the Father, so he who feeds on Me will live because of Me.

58   "This is the bread which came down from heaven—not as your fathers ate the manna, and are dead. He who eats this bread will live forever."

59   These things He said in the synagogue as He taught in Capernaum.

MANY DISCIPLES TURNED AWAY

60   Therefore many of His disciples, when they heard this, said, "This is a hard saying; who can understand it?"

61   When Jesus knew in Himself that His

disciples murmured about this, He said to them, "Does this offend you?

62 "What then if you should see the Son of Man ascend where He was before?

63 "It is the Spirit who gives life; the flesh profits nothing. The words that I speak to you are spirit, and they are life.

64 "But there are some of you who do not believe." For Jesus knew from the beginning who they were who did not believe, and who would betray Him.

65 And He said, "Therefore I have said to you that no one can come to Me unless it has been granted to him by My Father."

66 From that time many of His disciples went back and walked with Him no more.

67 Then Jesus said to the twelve, "Do you also want to go away?"

68 Then Simon Peter answered Him, "Lord, to whom shall we go? You have the words of eternal life.

69 "Also we have come to believe and know that You are the Christ, the Son of the living God."

70 Jesus answered them, "Did I not choose you, the twelve, and one of you is a devil?"

71 He spoke of Judas Iscariot, the son of Simon, for it was he who would betray Him, being one of the twelve.

JOHN 7

JESUS' BROTHERS DISBELIEVE

1 After these things Jesus walked in Galilee;

for He did not want to walk in Judea, because the Jews sought to kill Him.

2 Now the Jews' Feast of Tabernacles was at hand.

3 His brothers therefore said to Him, "Depart from here and go into Judea, that Your disciples also may see the works that You are doing.

4 "For no one does anything in secret while he himself seeks to be known openly. If You do these things, show Yourself to the world."

5 For even His brothers did not believe in Him.

6 Then Jesus said to them, "My time has not yet come, but your time is always ready.

7 "The world cannot hate you, but it hates Me because I testify of it that its works are evil.

8 "You go up to this feast. I am not yet going up to this feast, for My time has not yet fully come."

9 When He had said these things to them, He remained in Galilee.

THE HEAVENLY SCHOLAR

10 But when His brothers had gone up, then He also went up to the feast, not openly, but as it were in secret.

11 Then the Jews sought Him at the feast, and said, "Where is He?"

12 And there was much murmuring among the people concerning Him. Some said, "He is good"; others said, "No, on the contrary, He deceives the people."

13 However, no one spoke openly of Him for fear of the Jews.

14 Now about the middle of the feast Jesus went up into the temple and taught.

15   And the Jews marveled, saying, "How does this Man know letters, having never studied?"

16   Jesus answered them and said, "My doctrine is not Mine, but His who sent Me.

17   "If anyone wants to do His will, he shall know concerning the doctrine, whether it is from God or whether I speak on My own authority.

18   "He who speaks from himself seeks his own glory; but He who seeks the glory of the One who sent Him is true, and no unrighteousness is in Him.

19   "Did not Moses give you the law, and yet none of you keeps the law? Why do you seek to kill Me?"

20   The people answered and said, "You have a demon. Who is seeking to kill You?"

21   Jesus answered and said to them, "I did one work, and you all marvel.

22   "Moses therefore gave you circumcision (not that it is from Moses, but from the fathers), and you circumcise a man on the Sabbath.

23   "If a man receives circumcision on the Sabbath, so that the law of Moses should not be broken, are you angry with Me because I made a man completely well on the Sabbath?

24   "Do not judge according to appearance, but judge with righteous judgment."

COULD THIS BE THE CHRIST?

25   Then some of them from Jerusalem said, "Is this not He whom they seek to kill?

26   "But look! He speaks boldly, and they say nothing to Him. Do the rulers know indeed that this is truly the Christ?

27   "However, we know where this Man is from; but when the Christ comes, no one knows where He is from."

28   Then Jesus cried out, as He taught in the temple, saying, "You both know Me, and you know where I am from; and I have not come of Myself, but He who sent Me is true, whom you do not know.

29   "But I know Him, for I am from Him, and He sent Me."

30   Then they sought to take Him; but no one laid a hand on Him, because His hour had not yet come.

31   And many of the people believed in Him, and said, "When the Christ comes, will He do more signs than these which this Man has done?"

JESUS AND THE RELIGIOUS LEADERS

32   The Pharisees heard the crowd murmuring these things concerning Him, and the Pharisees and the chief priests sent officers to take Him.

33   Then Jesus said to them, "I shall be with you a little while longer, and then I go to Him who sent Me.

34   "You will seek Me and not find Me, and where I am you cannot come."

35   Then the Jews said among themselves, "Where does He intend to go that we shall not find Him? Does He intend to go to the Dispersion among the Greeks and teach the Greeks?

36   "What is this thing that He said, 'You will seek Me and not find Me, and where I am you cannot come'?"

THE PROMISE OF THE HOLY SPIRIT

37   On the last day, that great day of the feast, Jesus stood and cried out, saying, "If anyone thirsts, let him come to Me and drink.

38   "He who believes in Me, as the Scripture has said, out of his heart will flow rivers of living water."
39   But this He spoke concerning the Spirit, whom those believing in Him would receive; for the Holy Spirit was not yet given, because Jesus was not yet glorified.

WHO IS HE?

40   Therefore many from the crowd, when they heard this saying, said, "Truly this is the Prophet."
41   Others said, "This is the Christ," but some said, "Will the Christ come out of Galilee?
42   "Has not the Scripture said that the Christ comes from the seed of David and from the town of Bethlehem, where David was?"
43   So there was a division among the people because of Him.
44   Now some of them wanted to take Him, but no one laid hands on Him.

REJECTED BY THE AUTHORITIES

45   Then the officers came to the chief priests and Pharisees, who said to them, "Why have you not brought Him?"
46   The officers answered, "No man ever spoke like this Man!"
47   Then the Pharisees answered them, "Are you also deceived?
48   "Have any of the rulers or the Pharisees believed in Him?
49   "But this crowd that does not know the law is accursed."
50   Nicodemus (he who came to Jesus by night,

being one of them) said to them,

51   "Does our law judge a man before it hears him and knows what he is doing?"

52   They answered and said to him, "Are you also from Galilee? Search and look, for no prophet has arisen out of Galilee."

53   And everyone went to his own house.

JOHN 8

AN ADULTERESS FACES THE LIGHT OF THE WORLD

1   But Jesus went to the Mount of Olives.

2   But early in the morning He came again into the temple, and all the people came to Him; and He sat down and taught them.

3   Then the scribes and Pharisees brought to Him a woman caught in adultery. And when they had set her in the midst,

4   they said to Him, "Teacher, this woman was caught in adultery, in the very act.

5   "Now Moses, in the law, commanded us that such should be stoned. But what do You say?"

6   This they said, testing Him, that they might have something of which to accuse Him. But Jesus stooped down and wrote on the ground with His finger, as though He did not hear.

7   So when they continued asking Him, He raised Himself up and said to them, "He who is without sin among you, let him throw a stone at her first."

8   And again He stooped down and wrote on the ground.

9 Then those who heard it, being convicted by their conscience, went out one by one, beginning with the oldest even to the last. And Jesus was left alone, and the woman standing in the midst.

10 When Jesus had raised Himself up and saw no one but the woman, He said to her, "Woman, where are those accusers of yours? Has no one condemned you?"

11 She said, "No one, Lord." And Jesus said to her, "Neither do I condemn you; go and sin no more."

JESUS DEFENDS HIS SELF-WITNESS

12 Then Jesus spoke to them again, saying, "I am the light of the world. He who follows Me shall not walk in darkness, but have the light of life."

13 The Pharisees therefore said to Him, "You bear witness of Yourself; Your witness is not true."

14 Jesus answered and said to them, "Even if I bear witness of Myself, My witness is true, for I know where I came from and where I am going; but you do not know where I come from and where I am going.

15 "You judge according to the flesh; I judge no one.

16 "And yet if I do judge, My judgment is true; for I am not alone, but I am with the Father who sent Me.

17 "It is also written in your law that the testimony of two men is true.

18 "I am One who bears witness of Myself, and the Father who sent Me bears witness of Me."

19 Then they said to Him, "Where is Your Father?" Jesus answered, "You know neither Me nor My Father. If you had known Me, you would have known My Father also."

20   These words Jesus spoke in the treasury, as He taught in the temple; and no one laid hands on Him, for His hour had not yet come.

JESUS PREDICTS HIS DEPARTURE

21   Then Jesus said to them again, "I am going away, and you will seek Me, and will die in your sin. Where I go you cannot come."

22   So the Jews said, "Will He kill Himself, because He says, 'Where I go you cannot come'?"

23   And He said to them, "You are from beneath; I am from above. You are of this world; I am not of this world.

24   "Therefore I said to you that you will die in your sins; for if you do not believe that I am He, you will die in your sins."

25   Then they said to Him, "Who are You?" And Jesus said to them, "Just what I have been saying to you from the beginning.

26   "I have many things to say and to judge concerning you, but He who sent Me is true; and I speak to the world those things which I heard from Him."

27   They did not understand that He spoke to them of the Father.

28   Then Jesus said to them, "When you lift up the Son of Man, then you will know that I am He, and that I do nothing of Myself; but as My Father taught Me, I speak these things.

29   "And He who sent Me is with Me. The Father has not left Me alone, for I always do those things that please Him."

THE TRUTH SHALL MAKE YOUR FREE

30 As He spoke these words, many believed in Him.

31 Then Jesus said to those Jews who believed Him, "If you abide in My word, you are My disciples indeed.

32 "And you shall know the truth, and the truth shall make you free."

33 They answered Him, "We are Abraham's descendants, and have never been in bondage to anyone. How can you say, 'You will be made free'?"

34 Jesus answered them, "Most assuredly, I say to you, whoever commits sin is a slave of sin.

35 "And a slave does not abide in the house forever, but a son abides forever.

36 "Therefore if the Son makes you free, you shall be free indeed.

ABRAHAM'S SEED AND SATAN'S

37 "I know that you are Abraham's descendants, but you seek to kill Me, because My word has no place in you.

38 "I speak what I have seen with My Father, and you do what you have seen with your father."

39 They answered and said to Him, "Abraham is our father." Jesus said to them, "If you were Abraham's children, you would do the works of Abraham.

40 "But now you seek to kill Me, a Man who has told you the truth which I heard from God. Abraham did not do this.

41 "You do the deeds of your father." Then they said to Him, "We were not born of fornication; we have one Father—God."

42 Jesus said to them, "If God were your Father, you would love Me, for I proceeded forth and came from God; nor have I come of Myself, but

He sent Me.

43   "Why do you not understand My speech? Because you are not able to listen to My word.

44   "You are of your father the devil, and the desires of your father you want to do. He was a murderer from the beginning, and does not stand in the truth, because there is no truth in him. When he speaks a lie, he speaks from his own resources, for he is a liar and the father of it.

45   "But because I tell the truth, you do not believe Me.

46   "Which of you convicts Me of sin? And if I tell the truth, why do you not believe Me?

47   "He who is of God hears God's words; therefore you do not hear, because you are not of God."

BEFORE ABRAHAM WAS, I AM

48   Then the Jews answered and said to Him, "Do we not say rightly that You are a Samaritan and have a demon?"

49   Jesus answered, "I do not have a demon; but I honor My Father, and you dishonor Me.

50   "And I do not seek My own glory; there is One who seeks and judges.

51   "Most assuredly, I say to you, if anyone keeps My word he shall never see death."

52   Then the Jews said to Him, "Now we know that You have a demon! Abraham is dead, and the prophets; and You say, 'If anyone keeps My word he shall never taste death.

53   "Are You greater than our father Abraham, who is dead? And the prophets are dead. Whom do You make Yourself out to be?"

54   Jesus answered, "If I honor Myself, My

honor is nothing. It is My Father who honors Me, of whom you say that He is your God.

55   "Yet you have not known Him, but I know Him. And if I say, 'I do not know Him,' I shall be a liar like you; but I do know Him and keep His word.

56   "Your father Abraham rejoiced to see My day, and he saw it and was glad."

57   Then the Jews said to Him, "You are not yet fifty years old, and have You seen Abraham?"

58   Jesus said to them, "Most assuredly, I say to you, before Abraham was, I AM."

59   Then they took up stones to throw at Him; but Jesus hid Himself and went out of the temple, going through the midst of them, and so passed by.

JOHN 9

A MAN BORN BLIND RECEIVES SIGHT

1   Now as Jesus passed by, He saw a man who was blind from birth.

2   And His disciples asked Him, saying, "Rabbi, who sinned, this man or his parents, that he was born blind?"

3   Jesus answered, "Neither this man nor his parents sinned, but that the works of God should be revealed in him.

4   "I must work the works of Him who sent Me while it is day; the night is coming when no one can work.

5   "As long as I am in the world, I am the light of the world."

6   When He had said these things, He spat on the ground and made clay with the saliva; and He anointed the eyes of the blind man with the clay.

7　And He said to him, "Go, wash in the pool of Siloam" (which is translated, Sent). So he went and washed, and came back seeing.

8　Therefore the neighbors and those who previously had seen that he was blind said, "Is not this he who sat and begged?"

9　Some said, "This is he." Others said, "He is like him." He said, "I am he."

10　Therefore they said to him, "How were your eyes opened?"

11　He answered and said, "A Man called Jesus made clay and anointed my eyes and said to me, 'Go to the pool of Siloam and wash.' So I went and washed, and I received sight."

12　Then they said to him, "Where is He?" He said, "I do not know."

THE PHARISEES EXCOMMUNICATE THE HEALED MAN

13　They brought him who formerly was blind to the Pharisees.

14　Now it was a Sabbath when Jesus made the clay and opened his eyes.

15　Then the Pharisees also asked him again how he had received his sight. He said to them, "He put clay on my eyes, and I washed, and I see."

16　Therefore some of the Pharisees said, "This Man is not from God, because He does not keep the Sabbath." Others said, "How can a man who is a sinner do such miracles?" And there was a division among them.

17　They said to the blind man again, "What do you say about Him because He opened your eyes?" He said, "He is a prophet."

18 But the Jews did not believe concerning him, that he had been blind and received his sight, until they called the parents of him who had received his sight.

19 And they asked them, saying, "Is this your son, who you say was born blind? How then does he now see?"

20 His parents answered them and said, "We know that this is our son, and that he was born blind;

21 "but by what means he now sees we do not know, or who opened his eyes we do not know. He is of age; ask him. He will speak for himself."

22 His parents said these things because they feared the Jews, for the Jews had agreed already that if anyone confessed that He was Christ, he would be put out of the synagogue.

23 Therefore his parents said, "He is of age; ask him."

24 So they again called the man who was blind, and said to him, "Give God the glory! We know that this Man is a sinner."

25 He answered and said, "Whether He is a sinner or not I do not know. One thing I know: that though I was blind, now I see."

26 Then they said to him again, "What did He do to you? How did He open your eyes?"

27 He answered them, "I told you already, and you did not listen. Why do you want to hear it again? Do you also want to become His disciples?"

28 Then they reviled him and said, "You are His disciple, but we are Moses' disciples.

29 "We know that God spoke to Moses; as for this fellow, we do not know where He is from."

30 The man answered and said to them, "Why, this is a marvelous thing, that you do not know where He is from, and yet He has opened my eyes!

31   "Now we know that God does not hear sinners; but if anyone is a worshiper of God and does His will, He hears him.

32   "Since the world began it has been unheard of that anyone opened the eyes of one who was born blind.

33   "If this Man were not from God, He could do nothing."

34   They answered and said to him, "You were completely born in sins, and are you teaching us?" And they cast him out.

TRUE VISION AND TRUE BLINDNESS

35   Jesus heard that they had cast him out; and when He had found him, He said to him, "Do you believe in the Son of God?"

36   He answered and said, "Who is He, Lord, that I may believe in Him?"

37   And Jesus said to him, "You have both seen Him and it is He who is talking with you."

38   Then he said, "Lord, I believe!" And he worshiped Him.

39   And Jesus said, "For judgment I have come into this world, that those who do not see may see, and that those who see may be made blind."

40   Then some of the Pharisees who were with Him heard these words, and said to Him, "Are we blind also?"

41   Jesus said to them, "If you were blind, you would have no sin; but now you say, 'We see.' Therefore your sin remains.

JOHN 10

JESUS THE TRUE SHEPHERD

1 "Most assuredly, I say to you, he who does not enter the sheepfold by the door, but climbs up some other way, the same is a thief and a robber.

2 "But he who enters by the door is the shepherd of the sheep.

3 "To him the doorkeeper opens, and the sheep hear his voice; and he calls his own sheep by name and leads them out.

4 "And when he brings out his own sheep, he goes before them; and the sheep follow him, for they know his voice.

5 "Yet they will by no means follow a stranger, but will flee from him, for they do not know the voice of strangers."

6 Jesus used this illustration, but they did not understand the things which He spoke to them.

JESUS THE GOOD SHEPHERD

7 Then Jesus said to them again, "Most assuredly, I say to you, I am the door of the sheep.

8 "All who ever came before Me are thieves and robbers, but the sheep did not hear them.

9 "I am the door. If anyone enters by Me, he will be saved, and will go in and out and find pasture.

10 "The thief does not come except to steal, and to kill, and to destroy. I have come that they may have life, and that they may have it more abundantly.

11 "I am the good shepherd. The good

shepherd gives His life for the sheep.

12   "But he who is a hireling and not the shepherd, one who does not own the sheep, sees the wolf coming and leaves the sheep and flees; and the wolf catches the sheep and scatters them.

13   "The hireling flees because he is a hireling and does not care about the sheep.

14   "I am the good shepherd; and I know My sheep, and am known by My own.

15   "As the Father knows Me, even so I know the Father; and I lay down My life for the sheep.

16   "And other sheep I have which are not of this fold; them also I must bring, and they will hear My voice; and there will be one flock and one shepherd.

17   "Therefore My Father loves Me, because I lay down My life that I may take it again.

18   "No one takes it from Me, but I lay it down of Myself. I have power to lay it down, and I have power to take it again. This command I have received from My Father."

19   Therefore there was a division again among the Jews because of these sayings.

20   And many of them said, "He has a demon and is mad. Why do you listen to Him?"

21   Others said, "These are not the words of one who has a demon. Can a demon open the eyes of the blind?"

THE SHEPHERD KNOWS HIS SHEEP

22   Now it was the Feast of Dedication in Jerusalem, and it was winter.

23   And Jesus walked in the temple, in Solomon's porch.

24   Then the Jews surrounded Him and said to

Him, "How long do You keep us in doubt? If You are the Christ, tell us plainly."

25 Jesus answered them, "I told you, and you do not believe. The works that I do in My Father's name, they bear witness of Me.

26 "But you do not believe, because you are not of My sheep, as I said to you.

27 "My sheep hear My voice, and I know them, and they follow Me.

28 "And I give them eternal life, and they shall never perish; neither shall anyone snatch them out of My hand.

29 "My Father, who has given them to Me, is greater than all; and no one is able to snatch them out of My Father's hand.

30 "I and My Father are one."

RENEWED EFFORTS TO STONE JESUS

31 Then the Jews took up stones again to stone Him.

32 Jesus answered them, "Many good works I have shown you from My Father. For which of those works do you stone Me?"

33 The Jews answered Him, saying, "For a good work we do not stone You, but for blasphemy, and because You, being a Man, make Yourself God."

34 Jesus answered them, "Is it not written in your law, 'I said, "You are gods" '?

35 "If He called them gods, to whom the word of God came (and the Scripture cannot be broken),

36 "do you say of Him whom the Father sanctified and sent into the world, 'You are blaspheming,' because I said, 'I am the Son of God'?

37 "If I do not do the works of My Father, do not believe Me;

38   "but if I do, though you do not believe Me, believe the works, that you may know and believe that the Father is in Me, and I in Him."

39   Therefore they sought again to seize Him, but He escaped out of their hand.

THE BELIEVERS BEYOND JORDAN

40   And He went away again beyond the Jordan to the place where John was baptizing at first, and there He stayed.

41   Then many came to Him and said, "John performed no sign, but all the things that John spoke about this Man were true."

42   And many believed in Him there.

JOHN 11

THE DEATH OF LAZARUS

1   Now a certain man was sick, Lazarus of Bethany, the town of Mary and her sister Martha.

2   It was that Mary who anointed the Lord with fragrant oil and wiped His feet with her hair, whose brother Lazarus was sick.

3   Therefore the sisters sent to Him, saying, "Lord, behold, he whom You love is sick."

4   When Jesus heard that, He said, "This sickness is not unto death, but for the glory of God, that the Son of God may be glorified through it."

5   Now Jesus loved Martha and her sister and Lazarus.

6   So, when He heard that he was sick, He stayed two more days in the place where He was.

7   Then after this He said to the disciples, "Let us go to Judea again."

8   The disciples said to Him, "Rabbi, lately the Jews sought to stone You, and are You going there again?"

9   Jesus answered, "Are there not twelve hours in the day? If anyone walks in the day, he does not stumble, because he sees the light of this world.

10   "But if one walks in the night, he stumbles, because the light is not in him."

11   These things He said, and after that He said to them, "Our friend Lazarus sleeps, but I go that I may wake him up."

12   Then His disciples said, "Lord, if he sleeps he will get well."

13   However, Jesus spoke of his death, but they thought that He was speaking about taking rest in sleep.

14   Then Jesus said to them plainly, "Lazarus is dead.

15   "And I am glad for your sakes that I was not there, that you may believe. Nevertheless let us go to him."

16   Then Thomas, who is called Didymus, said to his fellow disciples, "Let us also go, that we may die with Him."

I AM THE RESURRECTION AND THE LIFE

17   So when Jesus came, He found that he had already been in the tomb four days.

18   Now Bethany was near Jerusalem, about two miles away.

19   And many of the Jews had joined the women around Martha and Mary, to comfort them concerning their brother.

20   Then Martha, as soon as she heard that Jesus was coming, went and met Him, but Mary was sitting in the house.

21   Then Martha said to Jesus, "Lord, if You had been here, my brother would not have died.

22   "But even now I know that whatever You ask of God, God will give You."

23   Jesus said to her, "Your brother will rise again."

24   Martha said to Him, "I know that he will rise again in the resurrection at the last day."

25   Jesus said to her, "I am the resurrection and the life. He who believes in Me, though he may die, he shall live.

26   "And whoever lives and believes in Me shall never die. Do you believe this?"

27   She said to Him, "Yes, Lord, I believe that You are the Christ, the Son of God, who is to come into the world."

JESUS AND DEATH, THE LAST ENEMY

28   And when she had said these things, she went her way and secretly called Mary her sister, saying, "The Teacher has come and is calling for you."

29   As soon as she heard that, she arose quickly and came to Him.

30   Now Jesus had not yet come into the town, but was in the place where Martha met Him.

31   Then the Jews who were with her in the house, and comforting her, when they saw that Mary rose up quickly and went out, followed her, saying, "She is going to the tomb to weep there."

32   Then, when Mary came where Jesus was, and saw Him, she fell down at His feet, saying to

Him, "Lord, if You had been here, my brother would not have died."

33 Therefore, when Jesus saw her weeping, and the Jews who came with her weeping, He groaned in the spirit and was troubled.

34 And He said, "Where have you laid him?" They said to Him, "Lord, come and see."

35 Jesus wept.

36 Then the Jews said, "See how He loved him!"

37 And some of them said, "Could not this Man, who opened the eyes of the blind, also have kept this man from dying?"

LAZARUS RAISED FROM THE DEAD

38 Then Jesus, again groaning in Himself, came to the tomb. It was a cave, and a stone lay against it.

39 Jesus said, "Take away the stone." Martha, the sister of him who was dead, said to Him, "Lord, by this time there is a stench, for he has been dead four days."

40 Jesus said to her, "Did I not say to you that if you would believe you would see the glory of God?"

41 Then they took away the stone from the place where the dead man was lying. And Jesus lifted up His eyes and said, "Father, I thank You that You have heard Me.

42 "And I know that You always hear Me, but because of the people who are standing by I said this, that they may believe that You sent Me."

43 Now when He had said these things, He cried with a loud voice, "Lazarus, come forth!"

44 And he who had died came out bound hand and foot with graveclothes, and his face was wrapped with a cloth. Jesus said to them, "Loose him, and let him go."

THE PLOT TO KILL JESUS

45 Then many of the Jews who had come to Mary, and had seen the things Jesus did, believed in Him.

46 But some of them went away to the Pharisees and told them the things Jesus did.

47 Then the chief priests and the Pharisees gathered a council and said, "What shall we do? For this Man works many signs.

48 "If we let Him alone like this, everyone will believe in Him, and the Romans will come and take away both our place and nation."

49 And one of them, Caiaphas, being high priest that year, said to them, "You know nothing at all,

50 "nor do you consider that it is expedient for us that one man should die for the people, and not that the whole nation should perish."

51 Now this he did not say on his own authority; but being high priest that year he prophesied that Jesus would die for the nation,

52 and not for that nation only, but also that He would gather together in one the children of God who were scattered abroad.

53 Then from that day on they plotted to put Him to death.

54 Therefore Jesus no longer walked openly among the Jews, but went from there into the country near the wilderness, to a city called Ephraim, and there remained with His disciples.

55 And the Passover of the Jews was near, and many went from the country up to Jerusalem before the Passover, to purify themselves.

56 Then they sought Jesus, and spoke among themselves as they stood in the temple, "What do you think—that He will not come to the feast?"

57 Now both the chief priests and the Pharisees had given a command, that if anyone knew where He was, he should report it, that they might seize Him.

JOHN 12

THE ANOINTING AT BETHANY

1 Then, six days before the Passover, Jesus came to Bethany, where Lazarus was who had been dead, whom He had raised from the dead.

2 There they made Him a supper; and Martha served, but Lazarus was one of those who sat at the table with Him.

3 Then Mary took a pound of very costly oil of spikenard, anointed the feet of Jesus, and wiped His feet with her hair. And the house was filled with the fragrance of the oil.

4 Then one of His disciples, Judas Iscariot, Simon's son, who would betray Him, said,

5 "Why was this fragrant oil not sold for three hundred denarii and given to the poor?"

6 This he said, not that he cared for the poor, but because he was a thief, and had the money box; and he used to take what was put in it.

7 Then Jesus said, "Let her alone; she has kept this for the day of My burial.

8 "For the poor you have with you always, but Me you do not have always."

THE PLOT TO KILL LAZARUS

9   Then a great many of the Jews knew that He was there; and they came, not for Jesus' sake only, but that they might also see Lazarus, whom He had raised from the dead.

10   But the chief priests took counsel that they might also put Lazarus to death,

11   because on account of him many of the Jews went away and believed in Jesus.

THE TRIUMPHAL ENTRY

12   The next day a great multitude that had come to the feast, when they heard that Jesus was coming to Jerusalem,

13   took branches of palm trees and went out to meet Him, and cried out: "Hosanna! 'Blessed is He who comes in the name of the Lord!' The King of Israel!"

14   Then Jesus, when He had found a young donkey, sat on it; as it is written:

15   "Fear not, daughter of Zion; behold, your King is coming, sitting on a donkey's colt."

16   His disciples did not understand these things at first; but when Jesus was glorified, then they remembered that these things were written about Him and that they had done these things to Him.

17   Therefore the people, who were with Him when He called Lazarus out of his tomb and raised him from the dead, bore witness.

18   For this reason the people also met Him, because they heard that He had done this sign.

19   The Pharisees therefore said among themselves, "You see that you are accomplishing nothing. Look, the world has gone after Him!"

THE FRUITFUL GRAIN OF WHEAT

20   Now there were certain Greeks among those who came up to worship at the feast.

21   Then they came to Philip, who was from Bethsaida of Galilee, and asked him, saying, "Sir, we wish to see Jesus."

22   Philip came and told Andrew, and in turn Andrew and Philip told Jesus.

23   But Jesus answered them, saying, "The hour has come that the Son of Man should be glorified.

24   "Most assuredly, I say to you, unless a grain of wheat falls into the ground and dies, it remains alone; but if it dies, it produces much grain.

25   "He who loves his life will lose it, and he who hates his life in this world will keep it for eternal life.

26   "If anyone serves Me, let him follow Me; and where I am, there My servant will be also. If anyone serves Me, him My Father will honor.

JESUS PREDICTS HIS DEATH ON THE CROSS

27   "Now My soul is troubled, and what shall I say? 'Father, save Me from this hour'? But for this purpose I came to this hour.

28   "Father, glorify Your name." Then a voice came from heaven, saying, "I have both glorified it and will glorify it again."

29   Therefore the people who stood by and heard it said that it had thundered. Others said, "An angel has spoken to Him."

30   Jesus answered and said, "This voice did

not come because of Me, but for your sake.

31   "Now is the judgment of this world; now the ruler of this world will be cast out.

32   "And I, if I am lifted up from the earth, will draw all peoples to Myself."

33   This He said, signifying by what death He would die.

34   The people answered Him, "We have heard from the law that the Christ remains forever; and how can You say, 'The Son of Man must be lifted up'? Who is this Son of Man?"

35   Then Jesus said to them, "A little while longer the light is with you. Walk while you have the light, lest darkness overtake you; he who walks in darkness does not know where he is going.

36   "While you have the light, believe in the light, that you may become sons of light." These things Jesus spoke, and departed, and was hidden from them.

WHO HAS BELIEVED OUR REPORT?

37   But although He had done so many signs before them, they did not believe in Him,

38   that the word of Isaiah the prophet might be fulfilled, which he spoke: "Lord, who has believed our report? And to whom has the arm of the Lord been revealed?"

39   Therefore they could not believe, because Isaiah said again:

40   "He has blinded their eyes and hardened their heart, lest they should see with their eyes and understand with their heart, lest they should turn, so that I should heal them."

41   These things Isaiah said when he saw His glory and spoke of Him.

42 Nevertheless even among the rulers many believed in Him, but because of the Pharisees they did not confess Him, lest they should be put out of the synagogue;

43 for they loved the praise of men more than the praise of God.

44 Then Jesus cried out and said, "He who believes in Me, believes not in Me but in Him who sent Me.

45 "And he who sees Me sees Him who sent Me.

46 "I have come as a light into the world, that whoever believes in Me should not abide in darkness.

47 "And if anyone hears My words and does not believe, I do not judge him; for I did not come to judge the world but to save the world.

48 "He who rejects Me, and does not receive My words, has that which judges him—the word that I have spoken will judge him in the last day.

49 "For I have not spoken on My own authority; but the Father who sent Me gave Me a command, what I should say and what I should speak.

50 "And I know that His command is everlasting life. Therefore, whatever I speak, just as the Father has told Me, so I speak."

JOHN 13

THE MASTER BECOMES A SERVANT

1 Now before the feast of the Passover, when Jesus knew that His hour had come that He should depart from this world to the Father, having loved His own who were in the world, He loved them to the end.

2 And supper being ended, the devil having already put it into the heart of Judas Iscariot, Simon's son, to betray Him,

3 Jesus, knowing that the Father had given all things into His hands, and that He had come from God and was going to God,

4 rose from supper and laid aside His garments, took a towel and girded Himself.

5 After that, He poured water into a basin and began to wash the disciples' feet, and to wipe them with the towel with which He was girded.

6 Then He came to Simon Peter. And Peter said to Him, "Lord, are You washing my feet?"

7 Jesus answered and said to him, "What I am doing you do not understand now, but you will know after this."

8 Peter said to Him, "You shall never wash my feet!" Jesus answered him, "If I do not wash you, you have no part with Me."

9 Simon Peter said to Him, "Lord, not my feet only, but also my hands and my head!"

10 Jesus said to him, "He who is bathed needs only to wash his feet, but is completely clean; and you are clean, but not all of you."

11 For He knew who would betray Him; therefore He said, "You are not all clean."

WE ALSO MUST SERVE

12   So when He had washed their feet, taken His garments, and sat down again, He said to them, "Do you know what I have done to you?

13   "You call me Teacher and Lord, and you say well, for so I am.

14   "If I then, your Lord and Teacher, have washed your feet, you also ought to wash one another's feet.

15   "For I have given you an example, that you should do as I have done to you.

16   "Most assuredly, I say to you, a servant is not greater than his master; nor is he who is sent greater than he who sent him.

17   "If you know these things, happy are you if you do them.

18   "I do not speak concerning all of you. I know whom I have chosen; but that the Scripture may be fulfilled, 'He who eats bread with Me has lifted up his heel against Me.'

19   "Now I tell you before it comes, that when it does come to pass, you may believe that I am He.

20   "Most assuredly, I say to you, he who receives whomever I send receives Me; and he who receives Me receives Him who sent Me."

21   When Jesus had said these things, He was troubled in spirit, and testified and said, "Most assuredly, I say to you, one of you will betray Me."

22   Then the disciples looked at one another, perplexed about whom He spoke.

23   Now there was leaning on Jesus' bosom one of His disciples, whom Jesus loved.

24   Simon Peter therefore motioned to him to ask who it was of whom He spoke.

25   Then, leaning back on Jesus' breast, he said

to Him, "Lord, who is it?"

26 Jesus answered, "It is he to whom I shall give a piece of bread when I have dipped it." And having dipped the bread, He gave it to Judas Iscariot, the son of Simon.

27 Now after the piece of bread, Satan entered him. Then Jesus said to him, "What you do, do quickly."

28 But no one at the table knew for what reason He said this to him.

29 For some thought, because Judas had the money box, that Jesus had said to him, "Buy those things we need for the feast," or that he should give something to the poor.

30 Having received the piece of bread, he then went out immediately. And it was night.

THE NEW COMMANDMENT

31 So, when he had gone out, Jesus said, "Now the Son of Man is glorified, and God is glorified in Him.

32 "If God is glorified in Him, God will also glorify Him in Himself, and glorify Him immediately.

33 "Little children, I shall be with you a little while longer. You will seek Me; and as I said to the Jews, 'Where I am going, you cannot come,' so now I say to you.

34 "A new commandment I give to you, that you love one another; as I have loved you, that you also love one another.

35 "By this all will know that you are My disciples, if you have love for one another."

JESUS PREDICTS PETER'S DENIAL

36 Simon Peter said to Him, "Lord, where are You going?" Jesus answered him, "Where I am going you cannot follow Me now, but you shall follow Me afterward."

37 Peter said to Him, "Lord, why can I not follow You now? I will lay down my life for Your sake."

38 Jesus answered him, "Will you lay down your life for My sake? Most assuredly, I say to you, the rooster shall not crow till you have denied Me three times.

JOHN 14

THE WAY, THE TRUTH, AND THE LIFE

1 "Let not your heart be troubled; you believe in God, believe also in Me.

2 "In My Father's house are many mansions; if it were not so, I would have told you. I go to prepare a place for you.

3 "And if I go and prepare a place for you, I will come again and receive you to Myself; that where I am, there you may be also.

4 "And where I go you know, and the way you know."

5 Thomas said to Him, "Lord, we do not know where You are going, and how can we know the way?"

6 Jesus said to him, "I am the way, the truth, and the life. No one comes to the Father except through Me.

THE FATHER REVEALED

7 "If you had known Me, you would have

known My Father also; and from now on you know Him and have seen Him."

8   Philip said to Him, "Lord, show us the Father, and it is sufficient for us."

9   Jesus said to him, "Have I been with you so long, and yet you have not known Me, Philip? He who has seen Me has seen the Father; so how can you say, 'Show us the Father'?

10   "Do you not believe that I am in the Father, and the Father in Me? The words that I speak to you I do not speak on My own authority; but the Father who dwells in Me does the works.

11   "Believe Me that I am in the Father and the Father in Me, or else believe Me for the sake of the works themselves.

THE ANSWERED PRAYER

12   "Most assuredly, I say to you, he who believes in Me, the works that I do he will do also; and greater works than these he will do, because I go to My Father.

13   "And whatever you ask in My name, that I will do, that the Father may be glorified in the Son.

14   "If you ask anything in My name, I will do it.

JESUS PROMISES ANOTHER HELPER

15   "If you love Me, keep My commandments.

16   "And I will pray the Father, and He will give you another Helper, that He may abide with you forever,

17   "even the Spirit of truth, whom the world cannot receive, because it neither sees Him nor knows Him; but you know Him, for He dwells with you and will be in you.

18   "I will not leave you orphans; I will come to you.

INDWELLING OF THE FATHER AND THE SON

19   "A little while longer and the world will see Me no more, but you will see Me. Because I live, you will live also.

20   "At that day you will know that I am in My Father, and you in Me, and I in you.

21   "He who has My commandments and keeps them, it is he who loves Me. And he who loves Me will be loved by My Father, and I will love him and manifest Myself to him."

22   Judas (not Iscariot) said to Him, "Lord, how is it that You will manifest Yourself to us, and not to the world?"

23   Jesus answered and said to him, "If anyone loves Me, he will keep My word; and My Father will love him, and We will come to him and make Our home with him.

24   "He who does not love Me does not keep My words; and the word which you hear is not Mine but the Father's who sent Me.

THE GIFT OF HIS PEACE

25   "These things I have spoken to you while being present with you.

26   "But the Helper, the Holy Spirit, whom the Father will send in My name, He will teach you all things, and bring to your remembrance all things that I said to you.

27   "Peace I leave with you, My peace I give to

you; not as the world gives do I give to you. Let not your heart be troubled, neither let it be afraid.

28 "You have heard Me say to you, 'I am going away and coming back to you.' If you loved Me, you would rejoice because I said, 'I am going to the Father,' for My Father is greater than I.

29 "And now I have told you before it comes, that when it does come to pass, you may believe.

30 "I will no longer talk much with you, for the ruler of this world is coming, and he has nothing in Me.

31 "But that the world may know that I love the Father, and as the Father gave Me commandment, so I do. Arise, let us go from here.

JOHN 15

THE TRUE VINE

1 "I am the true vine, and My Father is the vinedresser.

2 "Every branch in Me that does not bear fruit He takes away; and every branch that bears fruit He prunes, that it may bear more fruit.

3 "You are already clean because of the word which I have spoken to you.

4 "Abide in Me, and I in you. As the branch cannot bear fruit of itself, unless it abides in the vine, neither can you, unless you abide in Me.

5 "I am the vine, you are the branches. He who abides in Me, and I in him, bears much fruit; for without Me you can do nothing.

6 "If anyone does not abide in Me, he is cast out as a branch and is withered; and they gather them and throw them into the fire, and they are burned.

7 "If you abide in Me, and My words abide in you, you will ask what you desire, and it shall be done for you.

8 "By this My Father is glorified, that you bear much fruit; so you will be My disciples.

LOVE AND JOY PERFECTED

9 "As the Father loved Me, I also have loved you; abide in My love.

10 "If you keep My commandments, you will abide in My love, just as I have kept My Father's commandments and abide in His love.

11 "These things I have spoken to you, that My joy may remain in you, and that your joy may be full.

12 "This is My commandment, that you love one another as I have loved you.

13 "Greater love has no one than this, than to lay down one's life for his friends.

14 "You are My friends if you do whatever I command you.

15 "No longer do I call you servants, for a servant does not know what his master is doing; but I have called you friends, for all things that I heard from My Father I have made known to you.

16 "You did not choose Me, but I chose you and appointed you that you should go and bear fruit, and that your fruit should remain, that whatever you ask the Father in My name He may give you.

17 "These things I command you, that you love one another.

THE WORLD'S HATRED

18   "If the world hates you, you know that it hated Me before it hated you.

19   "If you were of the world, the world would love its own. Yet because you are not of the world, but I chose you out of the world, therefore the world hates you.

20   "Remember the word that I said to you, 'A servant is not greater than his master.' If they persecuted Me, they will also persecute you. If they kept My word, they will keep yours also.

21   "But all these things they will do to you for My name's sake, because they do not know Him who sent Me.

22   "If I had not come and spoken to them, they would have no sin, but now they have no excuse for their sin.

23   "He who hates Me hates My Father also.

24   "If I had not done among them the works which no one else did, they would have no sin; but now they have seen and also hated both Me and My Father.

25   "But this happened that the word might be fulfilled which is written in their law, 'They hated Me without a cause.'

THE COMING REJECTION

26   "But when the Helper comes, whom I shall send to you from the Father, the Spirit of truth who proceeds from the Father, He will testify of Me.

27   "And you also will bear witness, because you have been with Me from the beginning.

JOHN 16

1 "These things I have spoken to you, that you should not be made to stumble.

2 "They will put you out of the synagogues; yes, the time is coming that whoever kills you will think that he offers God service.

3 "And these things they will do to you because they have not known the Father nor Me.

4 "But these things I have told you, that when the time comes, you may remember that I told you of them. And these things I did not say to you at the beginning, because I was with you.

THE WORK OF THE HOLY SPIRIT

5 "But now I go away to Him who sent Me, and none of you asks Me, 'Where are You going?'

6 "But because I have said these things to you, sorrow has filled your heart.

7 "Nevertheless I tell you the truth. It is to your advantage that I go away; for if I do not go away, the Helper will not come to you; but if I depart, I will send Him to you.

8 "And when He has come, He will convict the world of sin, and of righteousness, and of judgment:

9 "of sin, because they do not believe Me;

10 "of righteousness, because I go to My Father and you see Me no more;

11 "of judgment, because the ruler of this world is judged.

12 "I still have many things to say to you, but you cannot bear them now.

13 "However, when He, the Spirit of truth, has

come, He will guide you into all truth; for He will not speak on His own authority, but whatever He hears He will speak; and He will tell you things to come.

14 "He will glorify Me, for He will take of what is Mine and declare it to you.

15 "All things that the Father has are Mine. Therefore I said that He will take of Mine and declare it to you.

SORROW WILL TURN TO JOY

16 "A little while, and you will not see Me; and again a little while, and you will see Me, because I go to the Father."

17 Then some of His disciples said among themselves, "What is this that He says to us, 'A little while, and you will not see Me; and again a little while, and you will see Me'; and, 'because I go to the Father'?"

18 They said therefore, "What is this that He says, 'A little while'? We do not know what He is saying."

19 Now Jesus knew that they desired to ask Him, and He said to them, "Are you inquiring among yourselves about what I said, 'A little while, and you will not see Me; and again a little while, and you will see Me'?

20 "Most assuredly, I say to you that you will weep and lament, but the world will rejoice; and you will be sorrowful, but your sorrow will be turned into joy.

21 "A woman, when she is in labor, has sorrow because her hour has come; but as soon as she has given birth to the child, she no longer remembers the anguish, for joy that a human being has been born into the world.

22 "Therefore you now have sorrow; but I will see you again and your heart will rejoice, and your joy no one will take from you.

23 "And in that day you will ask Me nothing. Most assuredly, I say to you, whatever you ask the Father in My name He will give you.

24 "Until now you have asked nothing in My name. Ask, and you will receive, that your joy may be full.

JESUS CHRIST HAS OVERCOME THE WORLD

25 "These things I have spoken to you in figurative language; but the time is coming when I will no longer speak to you in figurative language, but I will tell you plainly about the Father.

26 "In that day you will ask in My name, and I do not say to you that I shall pray the Father for you;

27 "for the Father Himself loves you, because you have loved Me, and have believed that I came forth from God.

28 "I came forth from the Father and have come into the world. Again, I leave the world and go to the Father."

29 His disciples said to Him, "See, now You are speaking plainly, and using no figure of speech!

30 "Now we are sure that You know all things, and have no need that anyone should question You. By this we believe that You came forth from God."

31 Jesus answered them, "Do you now believe?

32 "Indeed the hour is coming, yes, has now come, that you will be scattered, each to his own, and will leave Me alone. And yet I am not alone, because the Father is with Me.

33 "These things I have spoken to you, that in

Me you may have peace. In the world you will have tribulation; but be of good cheer, I have overcome the world."

JOHN 17

JESUS PRAYS FOR HIMSELF

1 Jesus spoke these words, lifted up His eyes to heaven, and said: "Father, the hour has come. Glorify Your Son, that Your Son also may glorify You,

2 "as You have given Him authority over all flesh, that He should give eternal life to as many as You have given Him.

3 "And this is eternal life, that they may know You, the only true God, and Jesus Christ whom You have sent.

4 "I have glorified You on the earth. I have finished the work which You have given Me to do.

5 "And now, O Father, glorify Me together with Yourself, with the glory which I had with You before the world was.

JESUS PRAYS FOR HIS DISCIPLES

6 "I have manifested Your name to the men whom You have given Me out of the world. They were Yours, You gave them to Me, and they have kept Your word

7 "Now they have known that all things which You have given Me are from You.

8 "For I have given to them the words which You have given Me; and they have received them, and have known surely that I came forth from You;

and they have believed that You sent Me.

9   "I pray for them. I do not pray for the world but for those whom You have given Me, for they are Yours.

10   "And all Mine are Yours, and Yours are Mine, and I am glorified in them.

11   "Now I am no longer in the world, but these are in the world, and I come to You. Holy Father, keep through Your name those whom You have given Me, that they may be one as We are.

12   "While I was with them in the world, I kept them in Your name. Those whom You gave Me I have kept; and none of them is lost except the son of perdition, that the Scripture might be fulfilled.

13   "But now I come to You, and these things I speak in the world, that they may have My joy fulfilled in themselves.

14   "I have given them Your word; and the world has hated them because they are not of the world, just as I am not of the world.

15   "I do not pray that You should take them out of the world, but that You should keep them from the evil one.

16   "They are not of the world, just as I am not of the world.

17   "Sanctify them by Your truth. Your word is truth.

18   "As You sent Me into the world, I also have sent them into the world.

19   "And for their sakes I sanctify Myself, that they also may be sanctified by the truth.

JESUS PRAYS FOR ALL BELIEVERS

20   "I do not pray for these alone, but also for those who will believe in Me through their word;

21 "that they all may be one, as You, Father, are in Me, and I in You; that they also may be one in Us, that the world may believe that You sent Me.

22 "And the glory which You gave Me I have given them, that they may be one just as We are one:

23 "I in them, and You in Me; that they may be made perfect in one, and that the world may know that You have sent Me, and have loved them as You have loved Me.

24 "Father, I desire that they also whom You gave Me may be with Me where I am, that they may behold My glory which You have given Me; for You loved Me before the foundation of the world.

25 "O righteous Father! The world has not known You, but I have known You; and these have known that You sent Me.

26 "And I have declared to them Your name, and will declare it, that the love with which You loved Me may be in them, and I in them."

JOHN 18

BETRAYAL AND ARREST IN GETHSEMANE

1 When Jesus had spoken these words, He went out with His disciples over the Brook Kidron, where there was a garden, which He and His disciples entered.

2 And Judas, who betrayed Him, also knew the place; for Jesus often met there with His disciples.

3 Then Judas, having received a detachment of troops, and officers from the chief priests and

Pharisees, came there with lanterns, torches, and weapons.

4   Jesus therefore, knowing all things that would come upon Him, went forward and said to them, "Whom are you seeking?"

5   They answered Him, "Jesus of Nazareth." Jesus said to them, "I am He." And Judas, who betrayed Him, also stood with them.

6   Then—when He said to them, "I am He,"—they drew back and fell to the ground.

7   Then He asked them again, "Whom are you seeking?" And they said, "Jesus of Nazareth."

8   Jesus answered, "I have told you that I am He. Therefore, if you seek Me, let these go their way,"

9   that the saying might be fulfilled which He spoke, "Of those whom You gave Me I have lost none."

10   Then Simon Peter, having a sword, drew it and struck the high priest's servant, and cut off his right ear. The servant's name was Malchus.

11   Then Jesus said to Peter, "Put your sword into the sheath. Shall I not drink the cup which My Father has given Me?"

BEFORE THE HIGH PRIEST

12   Then the detachment of troops and the captain and the officers of the Jews arrested Jesus and bound Him.

13   And they led Him away to Annas first, for he was the father-in-law of Caiaphas who was high priest that year.

14   Now it was Caiaphas who gave counsel to the Jews that it was expedient that one man should die for the people.

PETER DENIES JESUS

15   And Simon Peter followed Jesus, and so did another disciple. Now that disciple was known to the high priest, and went with Jesus into the courtyard of the high priest.

16   But Peter stood at the door outside. Then the other disciple, who was known to the high priest, went out and spoke to her who kept the door, and brought Peter in.

17   Then the servant girl who kept the door said to Peter, "You are not also one of this Man's disciples, are you?" He said, "I am not."

18   And the servants and officers who had made a fire of coals stood there, for it was cold, and they warmed themselves. And Peter stood with them and warmed himself.

JESUS QUESTIONED BY HIGH PRIEST

19   The high priest then asked Jesus about His disciples and His doctrine.

20 Jesus answered him, "I spoke openly to the world. I always taught in synagogues and in the temple, where the Jews always meet, and in secret I have said nothing.

21   "Why do you ask Me? Ask those who have heard Me what I said to them. Indeed they know what I said."

22   And when He had said these things, one of the officers who stood by struck Jesus with the palm of his hand, saying, "Do You answer the high priest like that?"

23   Jesus answered him, "If I have spoken evil, bear witness of the evil; but if well, why do you strike Me?"

24   Then Annas sent Him bound to Caiaphas the high priest.

PETER DENIES JESUS TWICE MORE

25   Now Simon Peter stood and warmed himself. Therefore they said to him, "You are not also one of His disciples, are you?" He denied it and said, "I am not!"
26   One of the servants of the high priest, a relative of him whose ear Peter cut off, said, "Did I not see you in the garden with Him?"
27   Peter then denied again; and immediately a rooster crowed.

IN PILATE'S COURT

28   Then they led Jesus from Caiaphas to the Praetorium, and it was early morning. But they themselves did not go into the Praetorium, lest they should be defiled, but that they might eat the Passover.
29   Pilate then went out to them and said, "What accusation do you bring against this Man?"
30   They answered and said to him, "If He were not an evildoer, we would not have delivered Him up to you."
31   Then Pilate said to them, "You take Him and judge Him according to your law." Therefore the Jews said to him, "It is not lawful for us to put anyone to death,"
32   that the saying of Jesus might be fulfilled which He spoke, signifying by what death He would die.
33   Then Pilate entered the Praetorium again, called Jesus, and said to Him, "Are You the King of

the Jews?"

34   Jesus answered him, "Are you speaking for yourself on this, or did others tell you this about Me?"

35   Pilate answered, "Am I a Jew? Your own nation and the chief priests have delivered You to me. What have You done?"

36   Jesus answered, "My kingdom is not of this world. If My kingdom were of this world, My servants would fight, so that I should not be delivered to the Jews; but now My kingdom is not from here."

37   Pilate therefore said to Him, "Are You a king then?" Jesus answered, "You say rightly that I am a king. For this cause I was born, and for this cause I have come into the world, that I should bear witness to the truth. Everyone who is of the truth hears My voice."

38   Pilate said to Him, "What is truth?" And when he had said this, he went out again to the Jews, and said to them, "I find no fault in Him at all.

TAKING THE PLACE OF BARABBAS

39   "But you have a custom that I should release someone to you at the Passover. Do you therefore want me to release to you the King of the Jews?"

40   Then they all cried again, saying, "Not this Man, but Barabbas!" Now Barabbas was a robber.

JOHN 19

THE SOLDIERS MOCK JESUS

1	So then Pilate took Jesus and scourged Him.

2	And the soldiers twisted a crown of thorns and put it on His head, and they put on Him a purple robe.

3	Then they said, "Hail, King of the Jews!" And they struck Him with their hands.

4	Pilate then went out again, and said to them, "Behold, I am bringing Him out to you, that you may know that I find no fault in Him."

PILATE'S DECISION

5	Then Jesus came out, wearing the crown of thorns and the purple robe. And Pilate said to them, "Behold the Man!"

6	Therefore, when the chief priests and officers saw Him, they cried out, saying, "Crucify Him, crucify Him!" Pilate said to them, "You take Him and crucify Him, for I find no fault in Him."

7	The Jews answered him, "We have a law, and according to our law He ought to die, because He made Himself the Son of God."

8	Therefore, when Pilate heard that saying, he was the more afraid,

9	and went again into the Praetorium, and said to Jesus, "Where are You from?" But Jesus gave him no answer.

10	Then Pilate said to Him, "Are You not speaking to me? Do You not know that I have power to crucify You, and power to release You?"

11   Jesus answered, "You could have no power at all against Me unless it had been given you from above. Therefore the one who delivered Me to you has the greater sin."

12   From then on Pilate sought to release Him, but the Jews cried out, saying, "If you let this Man go, you are not Caesar's friend. Whoever makes himself a king speaks against Caesar."

13   When Pilate therefore heard that saying, he brought Jesus out and sat down in the judgment seat in a place that is called The Pavement, but in Hebrew, Gabbatha.

14   Now it was the Preparation Day of the Passover, and about the sixth hour. And he said to the Jews, "Behold your King!"

15   But they cried out, "Away with Him, away with Him! Crucify Him!" Pilate said to them, "Shall I crucify your King?" The chief priests answered, "We have no king but Caesar!"

16   So he delivered Him to them to be crucified. So they took Jesus and led Him away.

THE KING ON A CROSS

17   And He, bearing His cross, went out to a place called the Place of a Skull, which is called in Hebrew, Golgotha,

18   where they crucified Him, and two others with Him, one on either side, and Jesus in the center.

19   Now Pilate wrote a title and put it on the cross. And the writing was: JESUS OF NAZARETH, THE KING OF THE JEWS.

20   Then many of the Jews read this title, for the place where Jesus was crucified was near the city; and it was written in Hebrew, Greek, and Latin.

21 Then the chief priests of the Jews said to Pilate, "Do not write, 'The King of the Jews,' but, 'He said, "I am the King of the Jews." ' "
22 Pilate answered, "What I have written, I have written."
23 Then the soldiers, when they had crucified Jesus, took His garments and made four parts, to each soldier a part, and also the tunic. Now the tunic was without seam, woven from the top in one piece.
24 They said therefore among themselves, "Let us not tear it, but cast lots for it, whose it shall be," that the Scripture might be fulfilled which says: "They divided My garments among them, and for My clothing they cast lots." Therefore the soldiers did these things.

BEHOLD YOUR MOTHER

25 Now there stood by the cross of Jesus His mother, and His mother's sister, Mary the wife of Clopas, and Mary Magdalene.
26 When Jesus therefore saw His mother, and the disciple whom He loved standing by, He said to His mother, "Woman, behold your son!"
27 Then He said to the disciple, "Behold your mother!" And from that hour that disciple took her to his own home.

IT IS FINISHED

28 After this, Jesus, knowing that all things were now accomplished, that the Scripture might be fulfilled, said, "I thirst!"
29 Now a vessel full of sour wine was sitting there; and they filled a sponge with sour wine, put it on hyssop, and put it to His mouth.

30 So when Jesus had received the sour wine, He said, "It is finished!" And bowing His head, He gave up His spirit.

JESUS' SIDE PIERCED

31 Therefore, because it was the Preparation Day, that the bodies should not remain on the cross on the Sabbath (for that Sabbath was a high day), the Jews asked Pilate that their legs might be broken, and that they might be taken away.

32 Then the soldiers came and broke the legs of the first and of the other who was crucified with Him.

33 But when they came to Jesus and saw that He was already dead, they did not break His legs.

34 But one of the soldiers pierced His side with a spear, and immediately blood and water came out.

35 And he who has seen has testified, and his testimony is true; and he knows that he is telling the truth, so that you may believe.

36 For these things were done that the Scripture should be fulfilled, "Not one of His bones shall be broken."

37 And again another Scripture says, "They shall look on Him whom they pierced."

JESUS BURIED IN JOSEPH'S TOMB

38 After this, Joseph of Arimathea, being a disciple of Jesus, but secretly, for fear of the Jews, asked Pilate that he might take away the body of Jesus; and Pilate gave him permission. So he came and took the body of Jesus.

39 And Nicodemus, who at first came to Jesus by night, also came, bringing a mixture of myrrh and aloes, about a hundred pounds.

40　Then they took the body of Jesus, and bound it in strips of linen with the spices, as the custom of the Jews is to bury.

41　Now in the place where He was crucified there was a garden, and in the garden a new tomb in which no one had yet been laid.

42　So there they laid Jesus, because of the Jews' Preparation Day, for the tomb was nearby.

JOHN 20

THE EMPTY TOMB

1　On the first day of the week Mary Magdalene came to the tomb early, while it was still dark, and saw that the stone had been taken away from the tomb.

2　Then she ran and came to Simon Peter, and to the other disciple, whom Jesus loved, and said to them, "They have taken away the Lord out of the tomb, and we do not know where they have laid Him."

3　Peter therefore went out, and the other disciple, and were going to the tomb.

4　So they both ran together, and the other disciple outran Peter and came to the tomb first.

5　And he, stooping down and looking in, saw the linen cloths lying there; yet he did not go in.

6　Then Simon Peter came, following him, and went into the tomb; and he saw the linen cloths lying there,

7　and the handkerchief that had been around His head, not lying with the linen cloths, but folded together in a place by itself.

8   Then the other disciple, who came to the tomb first, went in also; and he saw and believed.

9   For as yet they did not know the Scripture, that He must rise again from the dead.

10   Then the disciples went away again to their own homes.

MARY MAGDALENE SEES THE RISEN LORD

11   But Mary stood outside by the tomb weeping, and as she wept she stooped down and looked into the tomb.

12   And she saw two angels in white sitting, one at the head and the other at the feet, where the body of Jesus had lain.

13   Then they said to her, "Woman, why are you weeping?" She said to them, "Because they have taken away my Lord, and I do not know where they have laid Him."

14   Now when she had said this, she turned around and saw Jesus standing there, and did not know that it was Jesus.

15   Jesus said to her, "Woman, why are you weeping? Whom are you seeking?" She, supposing Him to be the gardener, said to Him, "Sir, if You have carried Him away, tell me where You have laid Him, and I will take Him away."

16   Jesus said to her, "Mary!" She turned and said to Him, "Rabboni!" (which is to say, Teacher).

17   Jesus said to her, "Do not cling to Me, for I have not yet ascended to My Father; but go to My brethren and say to them, 'I am ascending to My Father and your Father, and to My God and your God.' "

18   Mary Magdalene came and told the

disciples that she had seen the Lord, and that He had spoken these things to her.

THE APOSTLES COMMISSIONED

19 Then, the same day at evening, being the first day of the week, when the doors were shut where the disciples were assembled, for fear of the Jews, Jesus came and stood in the midst, and said to them, "Peace be with you."

20 Now when He had said this, He showed them His hands and His side. Then the disciples were glad when they saw the Lord.

21 Then Jesus said to them again, "Peace to you! As the Father has sent Me, I also send you."

22 And when He had said this, He breathed on them, and said to them, "Receive the Holy Spirit.

23 "If you forgive the sins of any, they are forgiven them; if you retain the sins of any, they are retained."

SEEING AND BELIEVING

24 But Thomas, called Didymus, one of the twelve, was not with them when Jesus came.

25 The other disciples therefore said to him, "We have seen the Lord." But he said to them, "Unless I see in His hands the print of the nails, and put my finger into the print of the nails, and put my hand into His side, I will not believe."

26 And after eight days His disciples were again inside, and Thomas with them. Jesus came, the doors being shut, and stood in the midst, and said, "Peace to you!"

27 Then He said to Thomas, "Reach your finger here, and look at My hands; and reach your hand here, and put it into My side. Do not be unbelieving, but believing."

28   And Thomas answered and said to Him, "My Lord and my God!"

29   Jesus said to him, "Thomas, because you have seen Me, you have believed. Blessed are those who have not seen and yet have believed."

THAT YOU MAY BELIEVE

30   And truly Jesus did many other signs in the presence of His disciples, which are not written in this book;

31   but these are written that you may believe that Jesus is the Christ, the Son of God, and that believing you may have life in His name.

JOHN 21

BREAKFAST BY THE SEA

1   After these things Jesus showed Himself again to the disciples at the Sea of Tiberias, and in this way He showed Himself:

2   Simon Peter, Thomas called Didymus, Nathanael of Cana in Galilee, the sons of Zebedee, and two others of His disciples were together.

3   Simon Peter said to them, "I am going fishing." They said to him, "We are going with you also." They went out and immediately got into the boat, and that night they caught nothing.

4   But when the morning had now come, Jesus stood on the shore; yet the disciples did not know that it was Jesus.

5   Then Jesus said to them, "Children, have you any food?" They answered Him, "No."

6   And He said to them, "Cast the net on the right side of the boat, and you will find some." So they cast, and now they were not able to draw it in because of the multitude of fish.

7   Therefore that disciple whom Jesus loved said to Peter, "It is the Lord!" Now when Simon Peter heard that it was the Lord, he put on his outer garment (for he had removed it), and plunged into the sea.

8   But the other disciples came in the little boat (for they were not far from land, but about two hundred cubits), dragging the net with fish.

9   Then, as soon as they had come to land, they saw a fire of coals there, and fish laid on it, and bread.

10   Jesus said to them, "Bring some of the fish which you have just caught."

11   Simon Peter went up and dragged the net to land, full of large fish, one hundred and fifty-three; and although there were so many, the net was not broken.

12   Jesus said to them, "Come and eat breakfast." Yet none of the disciples dared ask Him, "Who are You?"—knowing that it was the Lord.

13   Jesus then came and took the bread and gave it to them, and likewise the fish.

14   This is now the third time Jesus showed Himself to His disciples after He was raised from the dead.

JESUS RESTORES PETER

15   So when they had eaten breakfast, Jesus said to Simon Peter, "Simon, son of Jonah, do you love Me more than these?" He said to Him, "Yes, Lord; You know that I love You." He said to him,

"Feed My lambs."

16   He said to him again a second time, "Simon, son of Jonah, do you love Me?" He said to Him, "Yes, Lord; You know that I love You." He said to him, "Tend My sheep."

17   He said to him the third time, "Simon, son of Jonah, do you love Me?" Peter was grieved because He said to him the third time, "Do you love Me?" And he said to Him, "Lord, You know all things; You know that I love You." Jesus said to him, "Feed My sheep.

18   "Most assuredly, I say to you, when you were younger, you girded yourself and walked where you wished; but when you are old, you will stretch out your hands, and another will gird you and carry you where you do not wish."

19   This He spoke, signifying by what death he would glorify God. And when He had spoken this, He said to him, "Follow Me."

THE BELOVED DISCIPLE AND HIS BOOK

20   Then Peter, turning around, saw the disciple whom Jesus loved following, who also had leaned on His breast at the supper, and said, "Lord, who is the one who betrays You?"

21   Peter, seeing him, said to Jesus, "But Lord, what about this man?"

22   Jesus said to him, "If I will that he remain till I come, what is that to you? You follow Me."

23   Then this saying went out among the brethren that this disciple would not die. Yet Jesus did not say to him that he would not die, but, "If I will that he remain till I come, what is that to you?"

24   This is the disciple who testifies of these things, and wrote these things; and we know that his testimony is true.

25   And there are also many other things that Jesus did, which if they were written one by one, I suppose that even the world itself could not contain the books that would be written.

AMEN.

HOPE
FROM GOD'S WORD . . .

BECOME FAMILIAR WITH
THE SUBJECTS THROUGH
REVIEW, AND MEMORIZE
THE SCRIPTURE PASSAGES.
YOU WILL FREQUENTLY FIND
USE FOR THEM.

AFFLICTIONS

Are often providential · Psalm 119:67,71,75
God will deliver · Psalm 34:19

ANXIETY

Is relieved through prayer · Philippians 4:6,7
Remember God cares for you · 1 Peter 5:7

ASSURANCE

Eternal life promised · John 3:16
You can be sure · 1 John 5:11-13

COMFORT

Jesus - the Good Shepherd · Psalm 23
He will never forsake you · Hebrews 13:5,6

DISCOURAGEMENT

Don't give up · Galatians 6:9
God will help and strengthen · Isaiah 41:10

EMPTINESS

Christ can satisfy · Psalm 107:8,9
He will fulfill your desires · Psalm 37:4,5

FORGIVENESS

Forgiveness and cleansing · Psalm 32:5
Promised · 1 John 1:9

GUILT

No condemnation · Romans 8:1
No sin too great · Isaiah 1:18

JUDGMENT

Everyone accountable · Romans 14:12
& Hebrews 9:27

LONELINESS

His presence promised · Hebrews 13:5,6
In His presence is joy · Psalm 16:11

SUFFERING

Suffering has profit · Hebrews 12:6-11
It deepens the faith · 1 Peter 1:6,7
It's to be expected · 1 Peter 2:19-23
God's grace is sufficient · 2 Corinthians 12:9,10

TEMPTATIONS

How to avoid them · Matthew 26:41
What causes failure · James 1:13,14

VICTORY

Is in Christ · Philippians 4:13
Your inner source · 1 John 4:4
Seek God's help · 1 Corinthians 10:13

WORRY

God will provide · Philippians 4:19
Have faith in Him · Romans 4:20,21
Claim His promises · 1 John 5:14,15

PROMISES
FROM GOD'S WORD . . .

GOD HAS GIVEN US
MANY TREMENDOUS
PROMISES THROUGHOUT
THE BIBLE. HERE ARE
JUST A FEW. STUDY
THEM AND APPLY THEM
TO YOUR LIFE.

GOD'S LOVE IS UNFAILING

Isaiah 54:10

GOD HEARS OUR PRAYERS

1 Peter 3:12

GOD CARES FOR US

2 Corinthians 9:8

WE ARE BLESSED IN CHRIST

Ephesians 1:3

GOD PROMISES PEACE

John 14:27

GOD PROMISES JOY

John 15:10-11

GOD PROMISES REST

Matthew 11:28

GOD IS WITH US

Deuteronomy 31:8

GOD GIVES WISDOM

James 1:5

GOD IS IN CONTROL

Romans 8:28

NOTES:

_____

_____

_____

_____

_____

_____

_____

_____

_____

_____

_____

NOTES: